C ckens on the Law

F om the Bristol Blitz to Cornwall and back again

JOHN BUDD

redcliffe

First published in 2001 by Redcliffe Press Ltd.,
81G Pembroke Road, Bristol BS8 3EA

Telephone: 0117 9737207

© John Budd

ISBN 1 900178 34 6

British Cataloguing-in-Publication Data.
A catalogue record for this book is available from the British
Library.

Typeset by Mayhew Typesetting, Rhayader, Powys and
Printed by Hackman Printers, Tonypandy, Rhondda

When the first bomb screamed down, the sky was already flushed with scarlet flashes and criss-crossed with searchlight beams that probed the night like stiff white fingers. We crouched in the tiny cupboard under the stairs, and sang hymns to drown the noise and because we believed in God like never before; and we watched the paraffin lamp on the whitewashed wall vibrate in time with the frightening crump of detonations somewhere out there in the awful darkness. The explosions terrified our infant souls, and we knew that the calamity that our parents had feared but pretended to ignore was now upon us, murderous and immediate.

Everything that happened in the year preceding that terrible night in November, 1940 had been merely play-acting. The ration books, the gas masks, the erection of bomb shelters, the appearance of air raid wardens wearing dark uniforms and a newly assumed air of authority; all those and a thousand other changes which had slowly invaded our lives following the declaration of war, were nothing more than gentle limbering up. This was the real thing. We were at war, and the bloodcurdling wail of the air raid siren was at last sounding in earnest. The serenity of our lives was suddenly smashed, and the pain was that much greater because we felt as though a good and happy life had turned treacherously upon us and savaged us without reason.

To my mother and father
who had nothing
and gave me everything

1

Bedminster was a suburb of Bristol. Some might say it was an unfashionable suburb, but we kids didn't know that. We were perfectly happy to call it our home, largely because we had not yet learned that some addresses were more socially desirable than others. Neither did we know that we were poor, because we knew nothing else and so could make no comparisons. We were quite happy with life anyway.

We lived in Catherine Mead Street, one of a web of similar streets and identical houses built originally for the families of labourers. At one end was the huge Wills' factory, a red brickwork palace, so large that it went unnoticed. We knew little about it except that it was the ambition of every school-leaver in Bedminster to get a job in "Wills", and that it paid its employees something called a "bonus" twice a year. Every spring and Christmas, on "bonus day", the shops in East Street were full of Wills' folk eager to spend their extra cash. Robinson's the paper factory also paid a bonus, and so did Mardon's, but never on the scale and with the style of W.D. & H.O. Wills. Neither did they give so much attention to the welfare of their workers, extending even to their health and education, so that to work for Wills' was generally regarded as being a prized life membership, culminating in sad farewells, a pension and a gold watch.

Our narrow street was cobbled and the front doors were only a few feet from the kerb. It led from Wills' to Dean Lane at the other end, describing a shallow curve on the way. On a corner half way down was Mr. Mayo's General Stores, which served us as a village shop. Mr. Mayo was a large and comfortable man, with a brown jacket and a grey apron tied around his waist, and jowls which hung down over his collar and tie. His heavy red face was topped with cropped grey hair, and he had a smile which inspired confidence with the ease of a bedside doctor. He knew everybody and retailing the gossip was as much part of his business as selling the groceries. He had a rare ability to listen, and even when he was weighing out the sugar in stiff blue bags or balancing the brass weights on one side of his scales against a scoop-full of potatoes on the other, he still managed to convey to customers that he was giving them his undivided personal attention. When he wasn't serving, he perched on a stool with his elbows on the counter, taking his weight. In front of his cramped counter was a double row of biscuit tins with glass tops so that customers could see what they were buying. On the shop door was a bell on a spring; it rang loudly whenever the door opened or closed. On one window was a tea advertisement for "Peter the Planter". It depicted a tanned and smiling young Adonis in a pith helmet, and Mr Mayo constantly reassured me that this was indeed the great cricketer Wally Hammond himself. I had many discussions with my father about the wealth of Mr. Mayo. It seemed to me that, since he was always putting cash into a wooden till that pinged when he shut the drawer, he must be always piling up money. Patiently my father pointed out that Mr. Mayo had to pay for the goods before he sold them; but I was never fully convinced.

At the Dean Lane end was our school, and the sawmill, and Chinny Pope's cycle shop, and Mr. Stenner's, the newsagent and undertaker. Alongside these were the bakery and the fish-and-chip shop, and a music shop, because those were days when most front rooms housed a piano that was actually played regularly. Here too was Bristol South Baths, where you could have a swim, or hire a soap and towel and take a hot bath. Next to the baths was the Dame Emily Smythe Park, with its wooden bandstand set in a large area of sloping tarmac and bordered with plane trees. The park was graciously provided by the Smythe family on top of their coal mine when it closed, as a gift to the neighbourhood and a tribute to those Bedminster men who had toiled in that pit for half a century.

Our school, St Paul's Church of England Infants' School, was the parish school of St Paul's Church on Coronation Road. We saw quite a lot of the vicar of St Paul's. He was a stubby, homely man who always seemed to be wrestling with some inner agony, the solution to which demanded most of his attention. He came on special Saints' Days, and was always there on Empire Day. With his snowy white cassock he would stand before us at assembly, the table in front of him draped with the Union Flag, and tell us how God, the King, and the British Empire were all inextricably linked, and how they all conspired together to make England a better place. We sang "I Vow to Thee my Country" and "God Save our Gracious

6

King", and then they let us have the rest of the day off, thus making enthusiastic young imperialists of us all.

Only yards away was the sombre, red-brick edifice of Holy Cross Roman Catholic Church. For many, this was a mystical and slightly sinister building, but for my mother it was the secret centre of her spiritual life. She was as devout a Roman Catholic as my father was a committed Congregationalist. Years ago she had concluded that God would listen to her from whichever angle she approached Him, so she became a Protestant and sang evangelical hymns with great gusto alongside my father in Penn Street Tabernacle. But at heart she never ceased to be a Catholic, and my father never knew how many times she would find an excuse to smuggle me into Dean Lane and slip secretly into the forbidding porch of Holy Cross Church. That was a threatening and alarming world to an impressionable small boy, alert and alive to new influences. My mother, small but determined, would push hard at the varnished brown door and we would creep reverently into an atmosphere of shadows and gloom. Just inside and set into the wall was a dish of water. It obviously contained something powerful, because it made my mother become all solemn, splash the waters onto her forehead and drop into a deep curtsey towards the dim far end of the church. There, lit by flickering candles, and blurred by the bluish haze which gagged at the back of my throat, was a huge statue of Jesus, nailed to the cross, with frighteningly life-like gouts of blood gushing from His hands and His feet. All around were icons to Mary in a blue cloak and carrying a child in her arms. Sometimes there were solitary figures kneeling in the wooden pews, heads bowed and hands clenched, eyes screwed tightly shut, silent and private, motionless and isolated in prayer. It worried me. I didn't feel I had come to see God. I felt I was taking a risk by being there, and if I didn't behave something terrible would happen to me. I just didn't understand what was expected of me. I mustn't whisper, or shuffle my feet, or pick up a hymn book, or point at anything. I knew that whatever I did would be wrong, and could be punished by a loud howl and a bolt of lightning from above. I dreaded these visits. I never tried resisting them; they were inevitable, like occasional visits to the barber. But I always felt a surge of relief when my mother decided it was time to go. She would face the front and make a farewell curtsey, whilst I would hop from one foot to another, and bend my knees anxiously, in a hopeless attempt to copy her. But I was never successful, and rapidly found myself back outside in the blinding daylight, and propelled homewards with my hand firmly gripped and my mother looking furtively about her.

September 3rd 1939 in Catherine Mead Street was a beautiful late summer day. Two days earlier Hedley Verity had taken 7 wickets for 9 runs as Yorkshire bowled out Sussex for 33 at Hove in the last county game for six summers. In the June of that year Wally Hammond, my personal hero, had scored his 150th century and his fourth triple hundred while scoring 302 against Glamorgan. But on this sunny morning we drifted into our tiny back gardens with the windows open so that we could hear Mr. Chamberlain's promised broadcast about the war which my parents said was certain to happen. The tight row of houses were separated at the rear by identical brick walls, which were waist-high to the grown-ups. It was extraordinary to notice that all the neighbours seemed to have the same idea. It was as if they wanted to come out and listen to the broadcast with the others, but at the same time were careful to remain grouped within the security of their own families. They waited in apprehension for the speech to begin, and as they waited they looked over the wall and nodded to a neighbour, or muttered quietly among themselves. The men were mostly collarless and in shirtsleeves. Some wore flat caps, and the women had pinafores tied around their middles. Untypically (for they were a generally confident people), they seemed uncertain, and unwilling to make much comment.

At eleven o'clock Mr. Chamberlain began to speak, and I heard his old and exhausted voice announce that this country was now at war with Germany. Immediately there was a yelp of joy from Kenny Morgan next door. He was older than me, a big and happy boy with a large face and a toothy grin, and for some reason the prospect of a war delighted him. He was immediately floored by his father who struck him back-handed across the face. Kenny fell to the ground, more indignant than hurt, and glared reproachfully at Mr. Morgan. "What's that for then?" he whined. But he knew, really. The Great War was still fresh in the memory of everybody. Barely twenty years earlier it had ground to a halt under the weight of the terrible carnage it had generated. Some of the men who had fought in it and survived were still only in their late thirties, and every family had its own tale of horror to tell and a list of its own dead and wounded to recount. The Morgans were no exception, and neither was my own family. Even the Boer War was only forty years distant, and several of my living relatives had seen action there in South Africa. Men, old in experience but not in years, sat outside their homes in the sunshine and trembled uncontrollably, eyes fixed on something in the distance. "Shell-shock," whispered my father sadly when I asked. They had their own terrible memories of war.

Mr Chamberlain had told us we were now at war, and, in quiet tones, the neighbours exchanged views briefly with each other, shook their heads sorrowfully, and filed back indoors to discuss more closely the personal and private implications of the announcement. I wandered into the street and met Duggie Marshall and Ossie Marshall and the rest of our gang. With furrowed brows we recycled the opinions of our elders, and put them forward as our own personal views of the situation. Duggie Marshall was the Chief. He was a tall, willowy lad, and somewhat older than the rest of us, so we mainly listened to him. But none of us could dream how cruelly our lives were about to be twisted, and distorted beyond anything we could imagine. Tomorrow is a long way away to a small boy. We dispersed at the more immediate call of our mothers, about to serve Sunday dinner.

2   I do not recall much about the days before we moved to Catherine Mead Street. I know we lived in Temple Street, a narrow terraced street next to the famous leaning tower of Temple Church, where my parents had been married. One or two recollections stand out sharply because of the impression they made. I must have been about three or four years old, because I remember my mother taking me to the nursery school for the first time. In a large classroom was a row of shiny rexine beds where we were meant to rest during the afternoon. I viewed the prospect with a great deal of suspicion, and I wasn't completely enthralled at the idea of dozing the afternoon away with about a dozen unknown kids of my own age around me. So I began to yell, and scrambled towards the exit. One of the helpers ambushed me and put me in an arm-lock.

"Lie down and wait for your Mum to come back," she hissed between her clenched teeth, as my boot found her ankle.

"I want to go home," I yelled, and rushed through the door and back up the road after my mother before I could be captured. No amount of cajoling could induce me to return that day or the next; but soon, promises turned to threats, and by the end of the week I was just a small boy, doing as he was told while he worked out the odds.

I vividly remember Temple churchyard, and the smell of cut grass, and my fascination with the man with the scythe. He wore no jacket and had his trousers tied with string above his ankles. With unbroken patience, he swept his blade to and fro in a smooth rhythm which gradually reduced the whole patch to tidy lines of fallen grass and undergrowth. White butterflies zig-zagged low in the sunshine, and I took off my jacket and chased after them until I got near enough to fling it over them. Then I carefully picked them out of my coat and put them into a jam-jar half full of dandelion leaves, so they wouldn't starve, and marvelled at the soft white dust from their wings where it smudged onto my fingers.

It was in this churchyard one day that I first experienced the bleaker side of life. Surprisingly I had managed to evade the vigilance of my mother, who was usually alive to the activities of her first-born. I remember entering the churchyard and noticing that a small tent had unexpectedly appeared. Ever inquisitive, I trotted along to see who was intruding into my territory. A young man was crouching at the entrance. He seemed very friendly, but my presence obviously disturbed him, and he kept looking anxiously from me into the interior of the tent and back again. There were two other men inside. The bigger one was lying on his back, propped on his elbows, and when he saw me he gestured to me to come in. I crept under the canvas, squatted down, and looked at him. The atmosphere was rancid and fetid with tobacco smoke; and the hot sun beating on the pale canvas of the tent made the air hot and heavy. The man's face was red and shiny and his teeth were dirty. His hair was greasy and he wore a grubby collarless shirt under a shiny black waistcoat. His companion balanced on one elbow and looked up at me with a wet cigarette in his mouth. He kept giggling and rubbing his boots together.

The first man seemed to be clutching something close to his body.

"Look at this, then," he said. I leaned towards him, intensely curious. "Go on, touch it," he invited, and shuffled himself towards me.

"What is it?" I asked suspiciously.

"It's a piece of wood. There you are, touch it," he offered again. I bent over to inspect whatever it was he was holding.

"It's not a piece of wood," I said with certainty, "It's your willy."

This provoked alarming snickers from all three. They laughed, and shoved each other playfully, and the man at the entrance kept slapping his thighs in delight at my bewilderment. I suddenly felt menaced, and I barged past them out of the tent and raced home. As I fled across the clean grass I could hear roars of horrid laughter following me, but they made no attempt to stop me, and neither did they force me to do anything. I must have looked scared and upset when I got home to the security of my mother's hug; but my memory fails me here because I don't remember being scolded, or indeed whether she reacted at all. No doubt this was because of the skills of counselling, which all mothers are born with. My mother must have used them effectively to bathe the wound before it festered, but I shall never know how close I was to being seriously harmed that day. The incident stayed with me for years, and even now it disturbs me sometimes, as it floats intermittently to the surface of my consciousness.

3 We moved house to Catherine Mead Street several years before the war began. I don't know why we moved into Bedminster, but I can guess that it was so that my mother could be closer to her only sister, who lived a few hundred yards away in British Road. Neither do I know how my parents shifted our belongings to our new house. No doubt they went alongside the Cut, with its muddy brown ooze of tidal water; across Bedminster Bridge, down Coronation Road and into Dean Lane where it meets Gaol Ferry Bridge. The bridge was built to allow Bedminster workers to cross the Cut into Bristol without using the ferry. The 150-year old gates to the gaol, with its huge iron door, were all that remained of the granite building which had been erected to lock up French prisoners in the Napoleonic wars. It was the scene of many a public execution, and thousands of locals turned out on a good day to see the sport. Rowing boats were used to fish out the drunken revellers who fell off the edge and into the stinking water at the sheer hilarity of seeing a fellow human being have his life suddenly terminated.

Probably a horse and cart were involved in the removal of the family to Catherine Mead Street, with perhaps the assistance of home-made handcarts, which were the main methods of cartage in those days. But I know that in a narrow, cobbled street of terraced houses, with two small rooms and a scullery downstairs, two bedrooms up above, and a toilet in the back yard, I was as happy as a young boy could be.

I was now as impressionable as any other young lad. My parents surrounded me with books and encouraged me to ask questions, which they answered as patiently and fully as they could, given the fact that they had both left school before they were fourteen. My father was always reading, and liked to declaim whole passages aloud, using different voices and dialects for each character. This was ostensibly for the instruction of my mother and me, but I suspect it was also because there was a touch of the ham actor in his make-up which came strangely from one from his terribly deprived background. He would turn up the pressure in the gaslights in our living room, the better to read his script. Those gaslights – and the white silky "mantles" that provided the light - always intrigued me. They often had to be replaced because they were so fragile. They were bought in small cardboard boxes, and for all their frailty, when screwed onto the gas pipe and assisted by a pretty glass shade, transferred a dangerous-looking blue jet into a luminous white of sufficient intensity to read by.

My imagination was boundless, and I and my new pals, Duggie Marshall, and Ossie, and Rodney and Derek and the rest, were able to transform Catherine Mead Street in an instant into the setting for any plot we cared to devise. Usually we were Cowboys and Indians. Our heroes were Ken Maynard, Gene Autry, Buck Jones and Hopalong Cassidy. I didn't like being Gene Autry, because he kept stopping in the middle of the action to produce a shiny guitar from nowhere and sing soppy songs to some woman or other. This wasn't very manly, I felt. Real cowboys didn't shave, and had at least two guns and a rifle, and wore big hats and neckerchiefs, and spurs, and rode horses which snorted and rolled their eyes, and responded immediately to secret signs and whistles known only to themselves and their riders. Catherine Mead Street was the prairie, and we rode it ceaselessly, holding imaginary reins in one hand and slapping our bottoms with the other as we ran, to produce authentic galloping noises as we chased after rustlers or Indians or other assorted crooks.

Sometimes we were policemen chasing robbers or bandits. We could be pirates, or secret agents, or soldiers fighting the Jerries, the Germans being residual villains from the Great War, and reliable foemen. We were Mounties, or gold miners, or Robin Hood and his Merry Men, or Tarzan fighting native impis, with all of us allowed to beat our chests and outdo each other in delivering our personal renderings of Tarzan's famous victory cry. In fact, we could conduct our various battles in any conceivable scenario, and that little cobbled street responded faithfully. Duggie was always the leader. He was jealous of his position, but I made him agree that I could be his second-in-command no matter what game we played. I persisted in this delusion, even when the rest of the gang ignored my orders completely when Duggie couldn't come out to play. They were more inclined to regard Ossie Marshall as Duggie's natural replacement. Ossie didn't mind anyway. He was not a

14

dedicated gang member, but he had an attribute which placed him out of the reach of the rest of us. His family lived in a flat on the first floor in East Street, and on their balcony they kept a monkey on a lead. When life got dull, someone would say "Let's go and look at Ossie's monkey." And we all raced into East Street and stood in a group, gawping at the antics of the little beast.

The cobbles made playing ball games difficult; but we played Test matches at Lords or the Oval, F.A. Cup Finals at Wembley, or tennis at Wimbledon. I was good at games, so (under the captaincy of Duggie) I was allowed to be Wally Hammond at cricket and Eddie Hapgood at football. Our equipment in any of these exercises was strictly home-made. Swords and knives and guns were easy to simulate if you were prepared to use some imagination; but cricket balls and footballs were a different matter. They usually came as special Christmas or birthday presents. They were highly treasured and entitled the owner to privileges which even the supremacy of Duggie could not challenge. Once we had a golf ball, an astonishing article since none of us had the slightest idea of what golf was. In any case, it quickly got us into trouble. No matter how careful you were, the golf ball seemed to have an excess of energy all of its own. It would bounce miles up into the air, and gather pace when it landed, and hurtle unpredictably in all directions. After several brushes with grown-ups, Duggie decided that a golf ball was not really an essential part of our equipment so we disposed of it in the customary manner. We lifted up a drain cover, dropped it down into the sewer, and let it wash away down into the Cut and out of our existence.

Money was a permanent problem. My father was a road sweeper and a dustman. He was frugal in all he did because frugality was the only way of life he knew. He didn't drink and could scarcely afford his ten Woodbines a day, so there was no point in asking him for anything. None of the others was any better off, so occasionally we felt the need to be entrepreneurial. At Christmas time we could make money easily by going from door to door, singing carols. Where rival entrepreneurs would go around and bellow "While shepherds watched" and slam the doorknocker immediately, we were a little more artful. We learned one or two carols right through, put young David Berry up the front – he of the cherubic face and the famously sick father – and firmly resisted the urge to knock until we were sure we had been heard. That way we scored heavily over the opposition.

Bonfire Night was also a money-spinner for us. Again we gave the matter a great deal of thought. While other lads were content to tie a paper mask to the top of an old coat and demand "a penny for the Guy" for their appalling effigies of Mr. Fawkes, we would carefully scrounge suitable garments, and borrow somebody's push-chair, and wheel around a Guy to be proud of. Once we persuaded David Berry to sit in the push-chair himself on the promise of a large share of the profits; but even the attraction of a couple of coppers couldn't keep him still long enough to be a convincing Guy.

Such brief forays into the world of capitalism were seasonal, although I did have one golden day when my father brought home a bag of conkers from the Downs, and I sold them for a halfpenny a dozen.

The games we played seemed to appear on our calendar regularly without explanation. Nobody could tell, for instance, how the marbles season came and went, and gave way to the hoop season; or why pea-shooters lost their attraction and suddenly we all played five-stones, or collected cigarette cards – "Generals" – and saw who could flick them the longest distance, or "peg the farthest". Suddenly whips and tops would appear, or we would play cats' cradle with a length of string, or play tunes on a comb-and-paper. Hopscotch, and knock-out-ginger, and weak-horse, and girlish games like Queenie-ball, all took their turn as the craze of the moment.

But "Pin-a pin-a-poppy-show" ("Don't let your mother know!") was a different matter. Properly organised it could produce real money. You carefully sieved out all your personal treasures, together with what you could scrounge from gullible relatives and friends, and put them up for sale on the pavement outside your house. You usually sat on the doorstep with your goods laid out on a blanket or a chair, and called out "Pin-a-pin-a-poppy-show; don't-let-your-mother-know". Nobody had any idea what the slogan meant, but everybody knew what was intended. Bartering was the core of the game; but swapping was permitted, if your customer had something you wanted. The procedure was always the same. The kids would arrive in ones and twos, and subject your wares to a close inspection, involving jeers of derision and exaggerated groans of disbelief at the prices demanded. The bargains would disappear like lightning, and the hard graft came when the dross was opened to offers. The script rarely changed.

"*How much?*"

"A ha'penny? For that? It's broke anyway."

"A farden then."

"I wouldn't give thee a farden for ten of they."

"Put'n back in the box then."

"I'll give 'ee tuppence for the whole box then."

"You can 'ave 'un for a thrupenny bit."

"An' you can keep'n for that, an' all."

"Go on then, tuppence."

"Go on, then."

Money was produced, counted, and pocketed, the goods collected, and the deal concluded, honour remaining intact on both sides.

4   It was after a Poppy Show that I had my first experience of a doctor being called out on my behalf. I came away with a marble, a blood-alley, which rated as a "sixer" in our games. That meant you had to hit it six times with a "oner", or three times with a "twoer", before you could win it. I put the marble in my mouth, and suddenly it was gone. I'd swallowed it. I was quite sure I would die. I ran screaming into my mother and told her. She immediately gave me an almighty smack across the shoulders, I suppose to dislodge it or make it come shooting back up the way it had gone. But the blood-alley was now beyond recall, and already winding its way through my intestines. I was certain I would pass out at any moment. Suddenly the world stood up on end and I found myself gazing in terror at the linoleum floor. My mother had me by the ankles and was shaking me like a doormat, expecting the obstacle to come rattling out at any second. In between vicious shakes and tender hugs she gave me a whack across the legs to remind me not to be so stupid next time. And I kept wailing and howling and generally making my last days on earth as noisy as possible.

Mrs. Berry from across the road suddenly appeared. She thrust a cautious head around the door, her eyes wide with curiosity. She was a tall, stringy woman wearing a long and rapidly unravelling cardigan over her pinafore, her slippers scuffing the floor. She was white and anxious, quite sure that I was being battered to death by my demented mother who, during brief respites from jerking me violently up and down, described my shortcomings in words that I had never heard her use before. Mrs. Berry brightened up, and turned her fertile mind to producing a series of helpful suggestions.

"Make 'im sick," she offered.

"How am I supposed to do that," replied my mother breathlessly, still waving me about like a flag.

"Get some salt water down 'im." Whether my mother was attracted by the cure or by the chance to draw a fresh breath for further attacks on my person, I'm not saying; but she let me drop onto the floor while she dashed into the scullery. She reappeared with a block of salt, a spoon, and a glass of water.

"How much do you reckon I should put in?" she asked, as though all this was an experiment in cookery.

"Give it 'ere," said the indomitable Mrs. Berry. She grabbed the ingredients and began scraping salt into the glass until it contained salt and water in equal quantity. "Drink this, boy," she commanded, and when I gagged on it she grabbed my nose and upended the glass into my gaping mouth. Down went the liquid and up came everything I had eaten that day. Both women gathered around the product and studied it with interest, while I howled afresh and tried to stop retching and heaving.

"I can't see no marble," said Mrs. Berry accusingly, her disappointment clear for all to see. "Can't see nuffink like a marble." She was obviously bitterly disappointed, and frowned narrowly at my mother as if she had been cheated. "Better run round to Mill Lane and call the doctor."

There were never any cars parked in our street, and when the doctor arrived in his little black vehicle, half the neighbourhood turned out to watch. He was long and bony, with a little moustache and domed forehead like a white marrow. He wore a hairy brown jacket and a patterned pullover. He was also a local cricketer of some repute; so naturally I felt he was a man to be trusted. Besides, he was a doctor, and every kid in our street knew that doctors and vicars and teachers were very special people and had to be called "Sir."

"Can you feel where it is?" he asked.

I wrinkled my brow, closed my eyes, and concentrated like a diamond cutter.

"Yes," I said at last.

"Where?" he growled impatiently, and I pointed hesitantly at my throat.

He snorted. "Wherever it is, it's not there," he remarked, and suddenly shoved two stiff fingers into my stomach. I shrieked and doubled up, and he nodded his bulbous head in satisfaction. He turned to my mother. "Don't let him use the toilet," he said. "Make him use the pot until it pops out."

So for two days, every time I needed to, I used a little tin pot, which was a relief in some ways, because our toilet was outside in

19

the back yard. After each performance mother inspected the contents and shook her head anxiously. Then, on a glorious morning, bliss was it to be alive. I asked mother for the pot. She placed it strategically on the floor by my bed, and waited with her arms folded. I crouched and strained and was suddenly rewarded by a loud "ping!" as the lost marble shot out and struck the bottom of the tin receptacle, emitting a pure note in the key of B flat major. I pulled up my pyjama bottoms and danced around happily, not only because the long vigil was over, but also because I could now have my blood-alley back. I reached into the pot to retrieve it, but was brushed aside by my mother who said I was disgusting and carried the pot and its contents into the scullery. After a suitable period of purification, the marble was returned to me, glistening and smelling of antiseptic. I don't believe I ever played marbles with it again; I had too much respect for the troubles it had been through.

That may have been my first experience of medical attention, but it was not long before the little black car was once again parked outside of our house, soon to be followed by a dark-windowed bottle-green ambulance. A small crowd gathered to watch.

Brian Bevan and I were playing inventors. He was solid and chunky, with thick legs and his short grey trousers pulled tightly against his chubby thighs. We were doing inventions, with a long piece of string tied to the doorknob and trying to shut the bedroom door from downstairs in the passage. I had been feeling hot and unwell all the morning, and red patches were now appearing on my body. I became aware that Brian Bevan had stopped pulling the string, and was looking at me with great interest.

"What's the matter with you, then?" he asked.

"What do you mean?" I replied, annoyed that he was staring so hard, as if I was some kind of freak.

"You're all red!" he said, and made a show of backing away from me as if he was in mortal danger of catching something horrible.

"I'm not," I said indignantly, but went to check my appearance in the mirror all the same. My face was blotched, and I couldn't stop scratching; I itched all over.

My mother took one look at me and ran round to The People's Dispensary in Mill Lane, for the doctor. This time he seemed far more concerned than when he had called to make my lost marble re-appear. He took off his hairy brown jacket, and I saw that he was wearing a pair of braces as well as a thick leather belt. He sat me down on the sofa, unbuttoned my shirt and produced a double length of red rubber pipe with a shiny metal disc on one end and ivory hooks on the other. He shoved the hooks into his ears and pressed my chest at various spots with the round bit. He thrust a thermometer into my mouth, held my wrist while he looked at his watch, and then rose to his feet.

"You're right," he said to my mother. "It's scarlet fever. All the kids are catching it. I'll call the ambulance."

"Where will they take him?" asked my mother, now very worried indeed.

"Ham Green," said the doctor. "That's where they all go."

Brian Bevan, solid and chunky, tried to look invisible and shuffled towards the door.

"Where are you going?" said the doctor in a loud voice.

"Home," said the startled young Master Bevan.

"You stay here for a bit," said the doctor. "You might have caught it. In any case you won't be allowed out until we know whether you have it or not."

The ambulance arrived. I was lifted onto a stretcher, covered with a red blanket, carried out and thrust in through the doors at the back while my mother hovered, red-eyed and anxious. The neighbours clucked and made sympathetic noises and told each other that Ham Green Hospital must be full up by now with kids with scarlet fever. For a few fleeting seconds I was the centre of attention, and I felt I should wave bravely but weakly to the crowd, to show them that I was bearing up well in the circumstances, and was grateful for their good wishes. But the feeling soon passed as the doors slammed shut and the ambulance pulled away on its seven-mile journey out in the countryside to Pill and the Ham Green fever hospital.

By now my whole body was a spiteful crimson. I had never been in a hospital before, and I was much taken by the nurses in their starched uniforms and little hats. The attraction evaporated rapidly when the medicine came, as thick and dark as my mother's mint sauce on a Sunday, and smelling like pure peppermint. I was then told to have a bath, and was carried into the huge echoing bathroom at the end of the ward. I was dunked in hot water, scrubbed with a thick chunk of green soap which produced no lather, fished out,

21

wrapped in a rough towel, and deposited back into my bed. Then the nurse who performed these operations shoved a thermometer down my throat, retrieved it and looked at it, gave it a hard shake, and retired to renew her strength and think up some fresh tortures.

I stayed at Ham Green for two or three weeks, sleeping much of the time, until the itching disappeared, my temperature dropped, and I was at last allowed a daily walk in the hospital grounds. I didn't see much of my parents. Travel between Bristol and Pill was difficult and expensive, so the hospital had devised a system of advising relatives of the progress of the patients. Each inmate was given a number, and, while the epidemic lasted, these numbers appeared each night in the *Bristol Evening Post*, under the heading "Positive" or "Negative." When you joined the "Negatives" you knew you were on the way to recovery; and you looked forward each day to having a "swab" wiped around your tonsils, knowing that the result would be checked as an indication of your progress.

We had one flurry of excitement while I was there. During the afternoon the nurses began to rush about with buckets and brushes and cloths, and everything was scrubbed and rubbed until it gleamed. The excitement reached a crescendo, and I ventured to ask a nurse what was happening. "Queen Mary," she whispered as she raced about her business.

At home I had a picture of the new luxury cruise liner, the s.s. *Queen Mary*, and whilst I realised that the village of Pill stood on the banks of the river Avon that flowed to Bristol, I felt certain that the *Queen Mary* would be far too big to make the journey. Nevertheless the idea fired my imagination, and I could imagine her, sailing perhaps as far as Gaol Ferry Bridge. It wasn't possible to see the river from the hospital, but I tried, and climbed onto the window-ledge and reached up to the latch. From this precarious position I was wrenched by the immensely powerful ward sister, whose uniform seemed to crackle as she hauled me down.

"What are you up to?" she roared.

"I want to see the *Queen Mary*," I snivelled.

"Too late; she's been and gone," said Sister.

"She can't have gone up and back in one day," I yelled. But Sister, as usual, was busy and herded me back to bed. Too late I discovered that I had been looking for the wrong Queen. Ham Green Hospital had just received a visit from Queen Mary, the

22

Queen Mother, and I had been looking out for a great ocean-going liner that might possibly have got into Avonmouth Docks but could never have sailed an inch towards Bristol, never mind navigating the infamous Horseshoe Bend.

At last I was home again, but I was still not free from the worrying perplexities of illness in an age when working people had to sort problems out for themselves. The "Dispensary" was still that mysterious building in Mill Lane where you went to obtain free medicine or help from a doctor if you had no money, as long as you could prove it. It was very puzzling.

Late one afternoon, Mrs. Berry rushed across the street and hammered, screaming, on our front door. My father, collarless and in his shirtsleeves and braces, went to let her in, and I heard the panic in her voice as she tried to explain something to him. Without pausing, he ran across the street into Mrs. Berry's house. I trailed behind him, and I heard my mother shouting at me and calling me back indoors. I didn't, and I saw my father, grim-faced, emerge into the street carrying David Berry carefully in his arms. He walked down towards Dean Lane, and I followed, together with two or three other lads, and Mrs. Berry falling in behind and sobbing into her apron. My father was now marching briskly, leaning slightly backwards to balance the weight of David, who was white and lifeless and had his eyes closed. On we went, nobody speaking, and Mrs. Berry weeping, until we crossed Gaol Ferry Bridge. I realised then that we were heading for the General Hospital. My father didn't pause longer than it took to order me outside onto the pavement. Then he disappeared into the side door of the hospital with the limp form of David hanging loosely in his arms, and the distraught Mrs. Berry shuffling behind him. We didn't have long to wait. My father soon reappeared, looking as sad as I had ever seen him. He was alone, and he wheeled around and strode back the way we had come without saying a word. We never saw David Berry again. Before I was put to bed that night, I did venture to ask what was the matter with him. I remember my father saying one word – "abscess", and I lacked the courage to press the matter. As I said my prayers that night, under the supervision of my mother, she said a special prayer for David Berry; and next day we paid one of our visits to Holy Cross Roman Catholic Church in Dean Lane and lit a candle for him.

I never knew what had happened to David Berry. Strange things happened in those days, which nobody bothered to explain. I shall always remember that bizarre procession to the General Hospital, led by my father, who, quite out of character, had suddenly become decisive and in charge of matters.

5

My father was one of the finest men I ever knew. He wore his hair cut short, and flattened with Brilliantine when he went to church or to practise with the Shaftesbury Crusade Male Voice Choir. His eyebrows were thick and luxuriant above his strong brown eyes. His smile was never far away, and his face always looked weather-beaten and healthy, which was not surprising since he spent every working day of his life out of doors. He was one of a large family born at the turn of the nineteenth to the twentieth century, and raised in the Penn Street and Philadelphia Street slums of Bristol. I don't believe he ever knew exactly how many brothers and sisters he had. In those days, if you had too many offspring, you could usually hand one or two over to friends or relatives without troubling the authorities with the paperwork. He could list about a dozen siblings, but their ages were separated by well over twenty-five years. My God-fearing tyrant of a grandfather christened his eldest son Alpha. My father was the last, the runt of the litter. Grandfather must have been pretty certain of this, so, with black irony, they called my father Edward Omega. Where his brothers and sisters had been huge and broad-shouldered, with hands the size of frying pans, he was short and wiry, though exceptionally strong. When the rest of his family left home, either to marry or join the army, my father was left alone with his widowed father. My grandfather was strong-minded to the point of bigotry. He was known to the police, not for any dishonesty, but for doing what he thought was the right thing. His nonconformist attitude earned him several short spells in prison. Once he politely asked a lady to remove her picture hat in the Gem silent cinema because it obstructed his view. She refused, so he immediately removed it for her, thus earning himself seven days. On another occasion he and an ex-soldier with whom he had had a few words, refused to give way as they walked towards each other on the pavement. He did this several times before the police arrived. They called him "Bill the Paralyzer", particularly when he threw two constables bodily out into the street when they came to question him without a warrant. He pretended to resent the title, but secretly he revelled in it. At the age of seventy they lost him, and he was discovered walking back to Bristol from Cheddar, fifteen miles away. He had gone to enquire about a job. In his youth he was a blacksmith on an estate in Hampshire. He married above himself, and his wife's parents made it financially possible for them to move swiftly to Bristol and out of their sphere for good.

They lived in a "court", where the density of population was measured in people per room. There was a pump and a toilet outside, and cockroaches and vermin inside. My father almost died when he was a child when they fumigated the sleeping quarters without realising that he was among those present. They sealed the doors and windows and left sulphur candles burning to kill off the vermin. Then someone discovered that the boy was missing, so they unsealed everything and hauled him out, half suffocated. It was mother who told me about my father's dreadful life, and then only in short bursts of brief reminiscences. He rarely mentioned it himself, except to smile bleakly at some of his father's exploits. He never spoke ill of his father, in spite of everything, and always referred to him respectfully as "The Guv'nor". My mother would tell me how he and his father existed on what the old man could make by mending clocks or making ladders. He could be brutal. He only gave my father an order once, and if he didn't respond immediately, he was beaten. But their rooms were spotless and cleanliness was a second religion for my father.

He managed to retain some of "The Guv'nors" habits, much to the chagrin of my mother, who had spent years in service and knew exactly how to behave. He poured his tea into his saucer to drink it, and blew into the cup to cool it. He took pinches of salt from the salt-cellar and sprinkled it on his food between thumb and first finger. And if his fingers became greasy, he just wiped them in his hair, explaining with his wicked smile that it "did the scalp good", whilst pretending to ignore my mother's cries of disgust.

His brothers and sisters were so much his senior that he had nieces and nephews a year or two older than he was. His best friend, Will, was his nephew, the son of his sister Minnie, and six months my father's junior. When he died of tuberculosis my father was shattered. I never heard him mention any other close friends. He went to Castle Green School where he learnt to read and write, worship God and revere the King and the Empire. He must have had a teacher who was also an artist, because he proudly showed me how to draw spheres and cubes, suitably shaded to make them look three-dimensional. They played cricket and football on the tarmac in St. Matthias' Park where the homeless slept, and were expected to quit school as soon as possible in order to bring money into the family.

His first job was as a messenger boy in Fulford's, a leather wholesale firm. He lost that when "The Guv'nor" took exception to a remark made about the state of my father's shoes. Grandfather went to see the boss, and suggested that if he was not satisfied he might like to buy the boy a new pair. Work was hard to obtain, and it was about this time that the unemployed were demonstrating violently in Old Market Street and being chased down the side streets by the police with truncheons drawn. (He was aghast, later on, when I said I wouldn't mind being a policeman. "Suppose we had no food and had to steal a loaf of bread just to live. Would you be prepared to arrest your mother or me?" The violence of his argument astounded me at the time.)

He got a job cleaning buses for the Bristol Omnibus Company. When he lost that he was out of work for two years, and queued up every day with others like him, presenting themselves for inspection each morning at the yard of the Transport and Cleansing Department of Bristol Corporation, happy to obtain any type of work. He was as smart as he could be with no money for clothes, and at last he caught the eye of Wally Hale whose unenviable job it was to cast an eye over the day's bunch of hopefuls, select some and reject the rest. He thought my father measured up well, and two years of being an ever-present at the gate signified a certain willingness to work, so he gave him a job as a lamplighter. From there he rose to become a dustman and a road-sweeper, in which capacities he served, as befitted his station in life, loyally, diligently, and without complaint until well after the war.

The Transport and Cleansing Department provided no protective clothing for its labourers. My father cut slits in a piece of car inner tube to make gloves to protect his hands from the worst of the heavy work. Time after time I remember him being called out at night, with no notice, to grit icy roads with a shovel from the back of a lorry. Those were the only occasions when I saw my father cry. He

27

gave in and wept from being frozen to his very intestines by the bitter cold, and from the pain of the returning circulation to numbed extremities.

My mother, better educated and more sophisticated than my father, told me about a rare occasion when my father lost his temper and became violent. When I was born, my mother wanted me to be accepted into the Roman Catholic Church; but my father would have none of it. He also was a devout Christian but worshipped as a Congregationalist, and although he tried to be tolerant, he had no intention of having me grow up as a Catholic. Consequently my mother's priest would not recognise me as having a religion, and told my mother quite plainly that if I were not baptized as a Catholic I would remain a bastard in the eyes of the Church. My father was prepared to let the matter rest there in the interests of family harmony, but my mother was deeply upset. When we moved to Catherine Mead Street she would not tell the priest our new address, and life continued with no mention ever made between my parents of their problems of religion.

There came a time, however, when my mother appeared more and more distressed. My father was anxious, but she always protested that there was nothing amiss. And then the truth emerged. My father's workmate was a Catholic, and when my father confided that my mother too was a Catholic, and preferred the priest not to know where we lived, the other man felt duty-bound to tell his own priest and give him our address. Week after week the priest secretly called when my father was at work, and did his best to persuade my mother to have me accepted into his faith. My mother always refused, but so ingrained was her Catholic upbringing that she could not escape an overpowering feeling of guilt, and not a little fear of the consequences of what she perceived to be her disobedience. Father came home from work one day and found her crying bitterly.

"What's the trouble?" he asked. She could hold it no longer, and told him how desperately worried the constant urgings of the priest was making her. He didn't hesitate. He pushed his bicycle from the back yard back up our narrow passageway and into the street. My mother guessed what was happening, but he just ignored her. He pedalled to the home of his workmate and knocked at his door. I imagine the man knew what was coming before my father said a word.

"Did you tell the priest what I told you in confidence about my wife?" he demanded.

"Yes, Ted; I had to. If I hadn't . . ." But then my father's bony fist hit him so hard that he flew back up the passage and lay on the floor in a daze.

"Keep your nose out of our business," said my father. Then he remounted his old bike and rode to the presbytery for an interview with the priest. I can only imagine what was said. My father always insisted that any clergyman, be he parson, vicar or priest, of any denomination, was a man chosen by God, and should be treated with respect. I don't know how much his theory stood up to practice that night, but he must have been quite persuasive because the priest never came again. The price my father paid was a good telling off from my mother when he got home that night, and no doubt an awkward hour or two at work next morning. When it came to knowing he was right and acting accordingly, there was a good deal of "The Guv'nor" in my father.

He felt he knew what was right when he joined the army without waiting to be conscripted. He was old enough to avoid war service, but to him his duty was perfectly clear. His brothers had served with distinction in the Great War, and it was his job to serve King and Country in this one, regardless of an increasing family and the fact that he was in his thirties. "Nobody is going to show me the white feather," he told my mother, and he was off to Yeovil and joined the Gloucestershire Regiment, like his brothers before him, and where his brother Bill had served as a warrant officer. He managed to go through the war without receiving so much as a lance corporal's stripe. When I asked him why not, he gave me a pitying glance and said I wouldn't understand. He knew his station in life, and it did not involve ordering other people about. I certainly did not understand at the time, but I am sure I do now.

There is no point in speculating about how my father would have developed if he had been born into a different environment. Some great men and women came from the slums of Penn Street and Philadelphia Street, but most people there started too far back in the race to win anything. When you are born into such squalor, it is a daily struggle merely to exist. It is a mighty task to climb above it; and to progress beyond that point requires exceptional qualities and extraordinary stamina, which most people just did not possess.

Drunkenness was a way of life where my father lived, although thankfully none of his family was tempted. On the rare occasions when he turned to reminiscing, he spoke in an alarmingly offhand manner of the bizarre people he grew up with, and of incidents which appalled me. There was Black Nell, the gigantic prostitute who terrorised her neighbours; and the pastor who ended his disastrous marriage to a shameless wife by drinking the acid from an accumulator battery and dying in agony whilst the neighbours looked on. He spoke in awe of the man who had his throat cut outside the pub, and whom he watched, sitting with a blood-soaked towel around his neck whilst the life ebbed out of him as he waited hopelessly for succour, which never came.

And there was Frank Fisher, the Kissing Burglar. Frank was a very powerful man and only one policeman could handle him. Frank respected this officer. Usually it was sufficient for him to walk into the pub and say "Come on, Frank, you've had enough," and Frank would follow him to the cells as meekly as a lamb. Otherwise it took three or four big men to restrain him, and Fisher enjoyed every moment of the battle. The accepted way of transporting a violent prisoner to the police station at Trinity Road was by strapping his hands and feet to a four-wheeled trolley and wheeling him into custody; the neighbours regularly cheered Frank lustily as he completed his regal progress on a Saturday night to the lock-up.

Fisher was only a petty villain, but one night, after a particularly heavy session in the local, he somehow found his way to gracious Clifton. Drunk as a lord, he forced a door, climbed the stairs, and found himself in a bedroom in the presence of a lady so terrified that she couldn't speak. He was no doubt as surprised as she was to be there, with several gallons of beer still sloshing about inside of him. He told the judge later that she seemed so beautiful that he offered to leave immediately if only she would give him a kiss before he went. The sight of Fred's ferocious face, an inch or two from her own, his eyes goggling and his breath stinking of stale beer, must have frightened her to the verge of insanity. Terrified, she supplied the kiss and Frank promptly toppled out of view through the open window. He fell thirty feet on his head into the garden, knocking himself out, and the police found him, staggering about in the road, dazed but otherwise intact. When he came to trial, the judge gave him five years hard labour on Dartmoor, and the local papers covered the whole affair under the heading "The Kissing Burglar."

My father never tired of describing the change which came over Frank when he was released from prison. Gone was the huge body and the outrageous personality. He was now stooped and thin, and suffering from tuberculosis. He spoke little, and only then, like other convicts, out of the corner of his mouth, to fool the guards because prisoners were not allowed to speak to each other. Nobody was afraid of Frank Fisher any more. He had no money, no home, and no chance of getting work. He died shortly after, a broken man.

All this my father saw and yet remained unaffected. Despite his brutal environment, he loved classical music. He once slipped through the emergency door into the Colston Hall without paying, to hear Isobel Bailey sing the soprano solos in *The Messiah*. He was captivated by her voice, and never forgot "the beautiful lady in the long blue dress". He joined the Male Voice Choir at Penn Street Tabernacle, and before long was perfectly at ease with the tonic sol-fah method of musical notation. He developed a glorious bass voice. He would never sing a solo; that would be too much out of character. But for years he carried the second bass line in the Tabernacle and the Shaftesbury Crusade Male Voice choirs. I found it harrowing to stand next to him in chapel and sing. He had natural harmony, gave every note its true value, and challenged the rest of the congregation to do likewise. He could be alarmingly thunderous, or as soft as a muted flute. He adored the Glasgow Orpheus Choir, and regarded them as the last word in perfection in using the human voice. He had no idea, of course, that when the war came he would find himself in the army, at Lerwick on the Shetlands, singing *The Messiah* with the Lerwick Musical Society. He could never quite grasp the fact that Professor Cooke, the con-ductor, was only a corporal, and yet demanded and got absolute obedience from officers and townsfolk alike. He found nothing amiss about the sentiment in one of the hymns he learnt as a boy – "The rich man in his castle, the poor man at his gate." To him, that was the correct order of things.

6   War had been declared, but not, it seemed, in Catherine Mead Street. Life went along much as usual, although no doubt our parents were shielding us from much of what was happening. I now had a young brother. He was born on May 6th, 1935, which was the silver jubilee of the coronation of King George V and Queen Mary. He was naturally named George, after the king, and Edward, after my father. Like all "Jubilee Babies" in the kingdom, he was given a little silver cup as a souvenir of the occasion.

We had tea fish every Friday for supper. My mother, like a good Catholic, insisted that we have fish on a Friday. "Tea fish" was something I could never come to grips with. When she went shopping at the Home and Colonial or David Greig's on a Thursday, she stopped at Bryan's the fishmonger's and watched as the assistant cut off a chunk of something which looked like a stiff white board hanging on a hook. She took it home and soaked it all night, and on Friday she boiled it. It cost next to nothing and had no taste, but it was fish, allegedly, and that was good enough for her.

Friday night was bath night, and we went through the same ritual every week, in a zinc bath in front of the specially stoked-up fire, taking good care not to lean back against the rim nearest the flames. That was the way to get burnt. From time to time my mother hurried in from the scullery with another kettle of hot water, shouted a warning, and topped up the bath before it cooled. When we had finished, she and my father would grasp the handles at each end, and manoeuvre the soapy water out into the back yard and pour it away. We had no bathroom, and it never occurred to me to wonder how my father managed to take a bath. I know that every night when I was put to bed, he would be shaving, with his shirt undone at the neck and tucked under his braces to keep it clear of the lather. My mother said that he shaved at night because it saved time in the morning; he had to be at work before seven o'clock each day, including Saturdays.

My father at his ablutions was a sight to behold. He carried them out from first to last in silence and wearing a heavy frown of concentration. He had a short, stubby shaving brush, and spread the shaving soap liberally from eyebrows to neck, and shaved it off with the care of an Old Master at work. The operation routinely concluded with a face-wash, which meant filling both palms with water and diving into them with much blowing and gurgling. Evidently, the efficacy of the wash was in direct proportion to the amount of water sprayed around the kitchen. My mother waited patiently as the process reached its usual explosive climax so that she could mop up the sea of excess liquid with her dish-cloth. Since his hair was now as wet as if he had been out in a thunderstorm, he took a comb and, with infinite concentration, administered a parting in the sparse, military-style haircut he favoured. Then he dismantled his razor, took out the blade and wiped it dry, and put the equipment carefully away until the next onslaught.

My father fought a constant battle against bad feet. He was forever tending his corns and his stone-bruises, and scraping away with deep concentration at the hard skin brought about by incessantly walking the streets pushing a stiff brush. He also had colossal hammer toes, which made his feet look deformed. His big toes pointed sharply upwards as the tendons pulled tightly on them. Years later, he maintained that his feet were never in better condition than they were during the war, when he wore army boots all the time.

We listened on the wireless to programmes like "Monday Night at Eight" and "In Town Tonight", when somebody kindly "stopped the Mighty Roar of London's Traffic" so that we could hear people being interviewed. At the Stoll cinema in East Street we never missed the Saturday morning "tu'ppenny rush", with its cartoons and the serial which we followed faithfully from week to week. On Friday nights my father would come home from work bringing a "surprise". Often it was "pinky-fruit", cut-price apples or pears, oranges or bananas that had become too ripe to sell at full price, but which were delicious when my mother cut off the rotten parts. Sometimes we had a bag of broken biscuits, unattractive to the discerning customer, but perfectly acceptable to us, particularly in the inevitable scramble to be the first to get at the chocolate bits.

Perhaps the imminence of the "real" war would have become more obvious if we had noticed the way small things changed. One night my father's surprise present came when he called into Woolworth's on the way home and brought us a game of darts and a dartboard. The darts were tipped with rubber suckers, which stuck to the target. We had seen this idea before, but this time the targets were different. The bull's-eye was the large, open mouth of a man with a little black moustache and hair plastered down over one eye. Then there was a fat man in a peaked cap sitting on an aeroplane. In fact, we were being invited to throw darts at a group of Hitler's bogeymen, while experiencing our first taste of war propaganda.

But it was the affair of my Uncle Fred's revolver which made me realise that life was now becoming more urgent and immediate. Uncle Fred was a hero of the Great War. He was my father's brother, and before dying of wounds on the Somme, he won the Military Medal, was commissioned on the field of battle, and was awarded the Military Cross for a string of heroic deeds which took up a large part of one page in the *London Gazette*. We had a big photograph of him in full uniform hanging on the wall, with his Sam Browne tight across his bulging chest. In the top of the wardrobe in my parents' room was his service revolver. It was dull black in colour, and very heavy. From time to time my father took it down and let me hold it. Once I asked him how many Germans Uncle Fred would have shot with it, and he grew angry and put it back into the wardrobe.

One day an announcement appeared in the *Evening Post* and was repeated on the wireless. Anyone who possessed any kind of firearm was to take it at once to the nearest police station and hand it over in return for a receipt. My father thought about it for a long time, and eventually made up his mind. On the following Friday, he and I walked up Redcliffe Hill to Prewett Street where he always paid his union dues. On the way back, we walked down to East Street and into Bedminster Police Station. The building looked like a grimy stone castle from the Middle Ages. It had battlements and embra-sures and arrow-slits, and a square central tower, no doubt to remind the hard men of Bedminster to behave themselves. We went through an iron gate and into the reception office. There was a large man with a dark blue tunic sitting at the desk. His face was round and shiny, and a cigarette was burning in an ashtray. His tunic had silver buttons with medal ribbons on the pocket, and his neck bulged out over the tight collar. He didn't look much like a police-man because he was sitting down and was not wearing a helmet. He stood up and looked startled when my father produced the revolver and said he supposed he ought to hand it over. The constable looked warily at the large and lethal-looking weapon, and agreed that it might be a good idea, at that. So my father exchanged that precious souvenir of the brother of whom he was so proud, in return for a piece of paper, which he studied carefully, folded, and put away into his top pocket. The policemen said he was sorry and shrugged in sympathy. My father just looked at him, and we walked home in silence. Young as I was, I felt that something heavy was hanging in the air, and I knew that my father could manage quite well without any comment from me. When we got home my mother looked at him, and she shared his sadness. She put her hand on his arm, and said "Did they want it, Ted?" My father brightened up and looked quite proud. "Of course they did," he said, "Of course they did. They were very pleased that I took it in. They said what a fine weapon it was. They said the officers would be falling over themselves to own it." I didn't exactly recall that part of the conversation, but nothing in the world would ever make me admit it.

7 This was about the time that our fears began to amount to certainty that the war was about to catch up with us. A gang of workmen arrived and commenced activities in our school playground. We stood and watched them during breaks, and eventually the teacher told us that they were building an air-raid shelter. It took some time to construct, and we watched with growing curiosity as it took shape. There were no windows and it was dark and very badly lit. There were wooden benches down both sides, and we were taken into it and shown where to sit if there was an air raid. It was like a dark tunnel, and it smelt stale and musty, and we hated going inside. At one end the bricks in the wall were loose; the teacher said that was the emergency exit, and if we were trapped inside we had to scrabble the bricks away to get out.

Then they discovered it wasn't large enough to accommodate all the school at the same time, so the headmaster had a brainwave. He lined us all up, took out his notebook and a big watch, and told us all to rush home, touch our front door, and rush back again. This was a great game, and we all joined in the race. When we arrived back, breathless, at the school gate, he was there waiting and ticked off in his notebook how long it took us to reach home. He knew how many children the shelter would hold, and he had it worked out that the first couple of dozen youngsters who lived nearest the school, would not need a seat in the shelter because they had plenty of time to chase home when the air-raid siren sounded and before the bombs began to fall. Many parents, my own included, didn't think this was the best idea he had ever dreamed up, and told him so, but the rule stayed.

Then, as the summer began, paradise was brought to our very doorsteps by Bristol Corporation. Workers began building two brick shelters at the Wills' end of Catherine Mead Street. We had never had so much fun. Steel drums arrived and were quickly filled with water to be sluiced into the never-ceasing cement mixers to make mortar. A chemist among us, a genius in the making, discovered that dry ice, liberated from the ice-cream bins outside of Woolworth's and dropped into the barrels, made the water steam and bubble as though it was boiling. Thousands of red bricks were stacked in huge slab formation for us to climb; and, above all, countless lorry-loads of sand appeared. We watched, speechless, as the backs of the lorries tipped upwards and the sand shot off at increasing speed, climaxing in a satisfying "woooooosh". There was so much sand they didn't know where to put it all. It was like the Sahara desert; we climbed the walls of the shelter as they rose higher and higher, and jumped, thigh-deep, into the mountains of sand. We built sandcastles. We rolled in it. We were the Foreign Legion defending Fort Zinderneuf. We were deserters fleeing into the desert. We were Touregs fighting the Legionnaires. We were delirious; it was as though they had brought Weston-super-Mare to our front doors, and all that was missing were the donkeys. As the shelters took shape they began to use sand to fill sandbags and stack them against walls, and against windows, and up against the Wills' buildings. Everywhere was sand, and hosepipes never stopped flowing with green-cool water for us to make lakes and channels and waterfalls and canals and whole oceans, if needs be. The sand got into our hair, our eyes, and our shoes. When we got home it was in our pockets and our caps and our socks. It was gritty in our eyes as we sighed happily to sleep. That summer was glorious; and the war was already nine months old.

We were not so delighted about the gas masks, however. We were instructed to attend at our schools in the evenings to have them fitted. Grown-ups had ordinary, cylindrical rubber masks with a curved eyepiece and a cardboard box with a strap. Young children had "Donald Duck" masks, with rubber beaks, presumably to make them look like toys and render them more acceptable. Babies had a kind of transparent cage with a rubber frame into which they could be inserted bodily. We now went to school with a gas mask over one shoulder and a box of "iron rations" in a similar box slung over the other shoulder. This contained food, which would keep, in case we were trapped in the shelter for any length of time. We told each other that if we were caught on the way to school without these twin boxes, we could be stopped by a policeman and taken to prison. Everybody in our class knew somebody who knew somebody who had been locked up.

As the threat of the real war grew closer, the anxiety of our elders increased and before long we turned our fertile minds to problems of government. We knew that Mr. Chamberlain had to go (we had heard our parents say so often enough), and we were told that someone called Churchill should take his place. So we thought we should help the process on a little. One morning we ganged up in the street, armed ourselves with tin cans and toy drums and ashbin lids, and began to demonstrate in support of Mr. Churchill (whoever he was). When we got to East Street we marched into Woolworth's chanting:

> Vote, Vote, Vote for Mr. Churchill,
> Turn 'ole Chamberlain out the land.
> If I 'ad a penny gun I would shoot 'im up the bum,
> An, 'e wouldn't come to England any more!

There was another version, where the weapon was a "tuppn'y roll" and its positioning in Mr. Chamberlain's anatomy became more imaginative. I don't know how much our spontaneous demonstration influenced the course of the war at a national level, but it didn't do much good for our standing locally. The Woolworth's branch manager was a large, alert man, very fit, with a bald head and a light grey suit. He was possibly also a Nazi, because he counterattacked immediately, drove us out into East Street with the greatest of ease, and threatened to bar us all for life. "Life" to a youngster still in the Infants' School, is too long a period to have any meaning, so the threat was an empty one. Nevertheless, as all good generals should do after a temporary setback, we withdrew with a display of dignity mixed with prudence.

So the real war crept closer, and with it came still more occurrences which to children made no sense at all. In East Street, almost at the end of our street, was an Italian ice cream parlour. The owners were one of the many Italian families which had found their way to Bristol and South Wales between the wars. All we knew about them was that they were very pleasant people who made and sold ice cream cornets and wafers; they had black hair and white teeth with gold fillings, and they never stopped smiling. To us they belonged in East Street; so we just could not understand why it was that one day a crowd gathered and began to throw stones at the ornate glass frontage of their café. They jeered at them and shouted "Mussolini" and told them to go back to where they came from. The police came and the crowd broke up, but not before the pavements were covered with stones and broken glass, and one of the Italians was taken by ambulance to hospital. The shop did not open again for ages, and as usual when presented with a problem of this magnitude, I consulted my father. He didn't agree with the trouble, but explained that we were at war with Germany and Italy, so the crowd thought they were being patriotic by smashing up the property of an Italian family. It would not be long before Hitler began to take a terrible revenge.

8

One day we went to Mr. Mayo's shop to spend our weekly penny pocket money and Mr. Mayo said he had no sweets to sell us. He looked tired and worried these days, and was growing less and less like the dependable hub around which the affairs of Catherine Mead Street revolved. He said that before long sweets would be rationed, and so would bacon and butter and sugar and many other things, as they were in the last war, and soon it wouldn't be worth keeping his shop open. There was liquorice root available in plenty, however, so we tried some. It was like a hard wooden twig with dried bark; it turned yellow as you chewed it, and left splinters in your mouth which wedged in between the teeth and tasted ghastly. Mr. Mayo shrugged his heavy shoulders as if he were bearing a yoke, and said things would get worse before they got better.

It was on one of these fruitless journeys to Mr. Mayo's shop that we realised at last how serious the war had now become. We were chattering loudly, and Mr. Mayo was frowning impatiently, when suddenly the door crashed open and sent the bell spinning and jangling wildly. A lady hurtled in and stood gazing about her in fright as if she didn't know where she was. She looked like a mad woman. She wore no coat, her eyes were wide and her hair stuck out like springs. She was sobbing and her hands clutched her elbows tightly into her waist to stop herself from shaking. She was hysterical. "They've sunk the *Hood* – all hands lost – and my boy was on board." Quickly the shop began to fill with distraught neighbours, trying to comfort her and at the same time pumping each other for more news. H.M.S. *Hood* was Britain's most powerful giant battleship, and the German ship *Tirpitz* had sunk her. Everyone seemed to know someone who was serving in her when she was sent to the bottom of the sea. We had been brought up to believe that the Royal Navy was invincible, and now it had been struck a mortal blow. We were too young to assimilate the details, but the whole atmosphere and the very attitude of people underwent a change from that moment on. As Mr. Mayo had predicted, things were about to get worse.

No one who ever heard air-raid sirens will forget them; and yet I have never heard them described adequately. There was no terror in our experience which could remotely compare to being awakened by them, from a deep sleep in a warm bed, with the brain barely alive, to hear the obscene whine of the devil's own warning as it began at the bottom of its awful musical scale and lifted itself ever upwards in a parabola of fiendish sound, only to sink gloatingly back into the depths, and start all over again. We were utterly and absolutely terrified.

For the first few nights nothing happened in the way of bombing. The searchlights exercised themselves furiously across the black sky, and we could hear the throb of engines somewhere in the darkness above us. In common with all the neighbours, and guided by newspaper articles, we had carried out "air raid precautions." We had glued long strips of sticky brown paper across the window panes to prevent flying glass. We left the windows slightly ajar to allow free passage to bomb blast. And every window was covered with a blackout curtain of some kind. These were checked obsessively by air-raid wardens looking in from the street and trying to detect the merest glimmer of light.

Duggie Marshall found this particularly disgusting. "I suppose the Jerries are up there," he said, "miles above the ground, in the dark, dodging the barrage balloons, with anti-aircraft shells exploding all around them, and one finds time to turn to his mate and says 'What-ho, Fritz; I think I just spotted a flash of light coming from behind the curtain in number 27 Catherine Mead Street. Be a sport and chuck a couple of thousand-pounders down on them, while I try to shake off these three Spitfires'."

Just as pathetic were my father's honest and dutiful attempts to follow official advice and turn our cupboard under the stairs into a place of safety against the might of the German Air Force. We were told that the staircase cupboard was the safest place in the house, but even I could see how ridiculous that was. The house, indeed the entire street, had about as much chance of surviving a direct hit as a row of matchboxes under the tracks of a tank. Nevertheless my father, as usual, obeyed orders. He cleared the coal from the cupboard, whitewashed the interior, and banged in a couple of nails to support two small paraffin lamps. We furnished it with two stools, an orange box, and some cushions and blankets, and we were ready to face Herr Goering and the Luftwaffe.

And at last the bombing began. Night after night we locked ourselves into that shelter, and heard the anti-aircraft fire, and felt the whole house tremble as bombs rained down. And the more the terror crashed around us, the louder we sang our hymns and prayed to God for protection.

We were quite certain that we could distinguish enemy aircraft from our own by listening to the throb of the engines. An unbroken hum meant it was one of ours, but a throb with an irregular beat was undoubtedly a Jerry. We got used to cowering down in unison as bombs whistled down. They really did whistle as they fell, and the whistle climaxed into a scream as they neared the target. The bombs, they said, were made so that they would scream, in order to frighten the women and children below. If that was so, they certainly succeeded. We were scared to death as we waited in terror to discover whether the next one was meant for us. We quickly recognised too, the distinctive noise of the anti-aircraft guns. They seemed to explode with a crack rather than a bang, the more so when the night was frosty and the sky was clear.

At last the "all-clear" siren would sound its gentler, purer, single sustained note, which brought blessed relief to all who heard it. We would go back to bed for what remained of the night, and my father would set off for work as usual. Shortly we would go to school; but not one of us could resist putting his head out of the door into the fresh daylight and gazing in apprehension up and down Catherine Mead Street to see if any house had failed to survive the night.

There was also the vital matter of looking for shrapnel next day. All of us had Oxo tins full of jagged chunks of machined metal, which had once been part of gun-shells. A particularly good find was the fin of an incendiary bomb. These were dropped by the thousand and usually burnt out completely, but the cylindrical flights, which guided them like the feathers on an arrow, were quite common and good currency in the secret schoolboy business of barter and swap. I actually found a whole bomb, in the dark, in the gutter in Murray Street. I didn't know quite what to do with it so I left it while I went for a walk and considered the possibilities. When I had convinced myself that my father would be overjoyed to find me carrying a live incendiary bomb into the house, I returned to collect it. It had gone, and I was robbed of my prize, or saved from destruction, I will never know which.

So far no real damage had been done to Catherine Mead Street but the bombing was causing problems in other directions. It was obvious that the school children were suffering from sleepless nights and often failed to arrive in the morning. School windows were smashed and needed repair. Teachers were finding it difficult to cope with their own domestic problems and still arrive on time ready for a day's work. So the ever-fertile brain of our headmaster devised the mobile teacher scheme to meet the problems. He organised the children into groups, and teachers were allocated in turn to the houses of the youngsters so that they could have two or three hours' tuition under their own roofs. It was strange, at first, to have a teacher in the front room, giving lessons to half a dozen schoolmates; but, like everything else in these new and bizarre circumstances, we soon adjusted and actually welcomed weeks when we only worked half days.

Gradually the bombing worsened, until we abandoned the false safety of the stair cupboard for the much greater security of the brick air-raid shelters in the street, and eventually the crypt below St Paul's Church. These nights of sharing an air-raid shelter with about twenty neighbours, often from six in the evening to six next morning, would remain as indelible memories in the minds of those who were there.

Six in the evening seemed to be the favourite time for the warning siren to come alive, and the neighbours stoically built their day around the certainty of the German bombers paying us a visit at about that time. They had already combined with each other to make the shelter habitable. There were two identical buildings alongside each other with a tiny gap between them, and before long people had settled into a routine and had automatically staked a claim for a place in one or other of the shelters. Each was equipped with three-tier bunks made of thin strips of metal nailed over a wooden frame to form six-inch squares. People provided their own blankets and pillows and cushions, paraffin stoves for heating and oil lamps for lighting. A heavy blanket was rigged across the entrance and there was some attempt to brighten the interior with draped curtain material. Someone had even donated a large square of crimson carpet, but it was soon taken up and removed when it was discovered that it soaked up the moisture that ran down the walls, and quickly became wringing wet. It was winter, and nothing could prevent the chill from outside permeating the interior of those brick buildings. Old ladies sat huddled in long overcoats and blankets, their shoulders drooping, dreaming their dreams. They seemed to shrink as they sat with closed eyes, oblivious to the devil's orchestra going full blast outside. The children wore their pyjamas under layers of shirts and pullovers. The air of excitement and novelty which helped us through the early days of the blitz gradually faded away, to be replaced by a feeling of resignation and a fearful apprehension of what terrors each night might bring. Sometimes very little happened, and folk talked the night away or dozed or made the children comfortable as they themselves shifted and wriggled and prayed for the dawn and the "all clear".

But sooner or later during those long nights, the bombers droned towards us and told us what war meant to helpless civilians who could do absolutely nothing except sit and pray that the next crashing explosion would not be the one that finished us all off for good. On those nights, the singing would grow to a crescendo as the trapped families tried to make a noise louder than the cacophony outside. The non-stop repetition of popular songs turned into community hymn singing, as atheists turned into Christians, and believers challenged their God to protect them for just one more night. Condensation streamed down the brick walls and lay in pools on the old linoleum which had replaced the porous carpet. The air was blue with cigarette smoke, babies wailed and the women were not the only ones who sobbed in terror. Air raid wardens usually stood at the entrance to the shelter, eyes narrowed, gazing at the sky, and stepping smartly back at a particularly violent explosion. Generally they darted from street to street in their navy blue semi-military uniforms and shiny helmets with the initials ARP stencilled across the front. They grew in importance as people depended on them for news of what was happening outside beyond the thick draped curtain. Often they were joined by soldiers home on leave, anxious to help.

I remember the feeling of sympathy which filled our shelter when a young man suddenly burst into the gloom, dazed and lost. He had been looking for his friend's family and had come to the wrong street. He was black with dirt and stunk of gas fumes where he had been blown into a bomb crater and had crawled out without the slightest idea of where he was. He stood, blinking in the dim light as the singing stopped and the shellfire grew more furious. Everyone wanted to help him. Hot drinks from vacuum flasks were thrust upon him, and people nudged up to make room for him to sit down and gather his wits. In spite of our efforts to dissuade him, he soon stumbled back out into the darkness and we never saw him again.

Sometimes you could hear the wardens whispering together. "Don't tell Mrs Jones, but number 86 has had it." And Mrs Jones went on singing heartily, unaware that her house had received a direct hit, and she was suddenly homeless.

Our turn soon came. By a miracle a small bomb missed the adjoining shelter by a foot or so, and landed in the static water tank alongside. People were hurt and taken away, but we did not know the extent of the damage to our shelter until next day, when a crack in the brickwork was found to extend all around the building, enough to make it too dangerous to use.

From then onwards we were sent every night to the crypt of St Paul's Church in Coronation Road, a few hundred yards away, where room was found for all of us in spite of the already severe over-crowding. The A.R.P. wardens were in charge, and somehow my family remained together despite the chaos. It was there that I realised how poor my family really was. On a frosty December evening, in the moonlight, as we made yet another weary journey from our home to the crypt, my father dropped a two-shilling piece in the road. We all stopped and helped him look for it, and didn't move on until we found it, despite the threat of the bombers. Two shillings (ten pence) was all the money my father had in the world until next pay day, and he dare not leave it behind.

St Paul's crypt was a far more impersonal refuge than our brick air-raid shelter. People were always coming and going, and in the early evening the neighbours filtered towards it like spectators making their way to a football match. It was available for anyone who was passing as well as the majority who slept there each night. I sometimes wondered why some of the young men and women who formed groups in the doorway, talking and smoking, would briefly disappear in pairs into the bushes surrounding the church; and why it was that the same ladies would be there most nights and would be especially interested in men in uniform. At least it was warm down

45

there, and the bombs didn't make so much noise unless a particularly big one landed close by. And when the God-sent "All
Clear" siren sounded, there was always a defiant cheer from those
present as they hauled themselves out of bed and prepared to
trudge homewards yet again.

9

Soon we were to make our last journey to the crypt. After a particularly violent night, when people seemed to be talking to each other more often and more anxiously than usual, we arrived home to find our little house in ruins. It was not flattened, as were two or three others in Catherine Mead Street. But the windows had disappeared, there were holes in the roof, the curtains were on the floor, and the water and the gas were cut off. Outside, as it grew lighter, it was apparent that others had suffered more than we had. The road was covered in debris and, down at the far end near the school, neighbours in two houses were scrambling over piles of rubble in an attempt to see what could be salvaged from the ruins.

My father didn't go to work that day. My mother made him take me to British Road to see if her mother and sister and their family had escaped that air raid. My father looked exhausted and more miserable than I had ever seen him. We turned the corner and picked our way around bomb craters filling with water and sewage and stinking of gas where the pipes had been cut. Fires had been built to get rid of smashed floorboards and doors and anything else which was beyond use, and the brisk flames and clean blue smoke contrasted strangely with the surrounding drabness. Nobody was at work; people were shovelling, or sweeping, or filling carts and lorries with pathetic pieces of ruined furniture and household goods, wrenched from the ruins to clear the way for the establishment of some form of order. Bomb blast had ripped away the front or the sides of some houses. Bedrooms were exposed to view, at an angle, but with wallpapered interiors which yesterday were private, now gouged open to public gaze. I was fascinated to see one house with a motor car wedged one floor up. The air of cheerful defiance we had grown used to had disappeared, in its place was a feeling of resignation.

A car tried to nose past through the rubble, and sent a half-brick flying at my father. It struck him in the thigh, and his reaction horrified me. He wrenched open the car door and had the terrified driver out and over the bonnet in an instant. But he rapidly calmed down, and apologised, and helped the man back into his car, and we went on our way to British Road in silence.

My Auntie Jessie and my Gran were safe but in tears, but my father was in no mind to comfort them. They were unscathed apart from the shock, whilst we had more than enough trouble to return to. Back we struggled, to Catherine Mead Street along Dean Lane where workmen were already performing miracles with nothing more than spades and pickaxes to clear what had once been whole houses. My parents spoke to the Bristol Corporation officials, and we were rapidly allocated another house. In fact, we had a choice of two; one in Knowle West and the other in the St John's Lane area of Bedminster. We had never been anywhere near either place, and I scarcely knew where they were.

So my comfortable, cosy little existence, which the war had long threatened to curtail, was now at an end. We left Catherine Mead Street with its cobbled road and the friendliness of Mr Mayo's shop, and Duggie and the gang, and Ossie and his monkey, and the mighty Wills' factory, and all the happiness I had known for most of my young life. All wiped out in the space of a few days, and we were transported, with what belongings we had left, to a council house in Lynton Road, Bedminster.

We had been "bombed out". We were still alive and uninjured, and had no debts, although all we had left in the world didn't even fill a corporation van. But if we thought Herr Hitler had finished tormenting us, we were badly mistaken.

1 & 2 The class of 1937: St. Paul's Infants' School, Dean Lane, Bedminster. The author is somewhere in the midde front row and, below, some pupils meet up again in October 2000. The author is sitting, bottom right.

3. The author's mother, Annie Budd, around 1930 when in service. On the reverse she had written: 'How do you like this? Don't you think I look like a governess or school teacher?'

4. The author's father, Edward Budd, reading, in his wartime posting to Lerwick, Shetlands.

5. Uncle Captain Frederick Budd, holder of
MM and MC, killed on the Somme, 1918.
The author found his grave in a British
cemetery near Cambrai.

6. Catherine Mead Street today, with the former Wills' building as a backdrop.

7. A typical 'back alley' into East Street, Bedminster, opposite Wills'
factory, 1980.

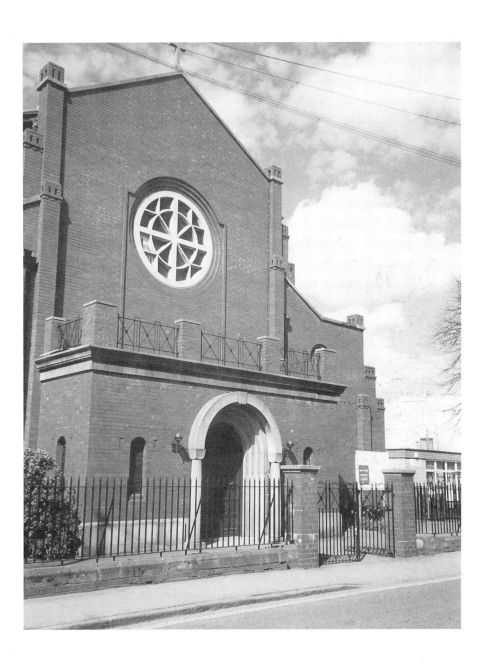

8. Holy Cross Roman Catholic Church, Dean Lane, Bedminster.

9. Philip Street Baptist Chapel, Bedminster, 1980.

10

Lynton Road was an estate of council houses built in the 1930s, mainly to take the families cleared from the dreadful slums in the centre of Bristol, where my mother and father had grown up. It was totally unlike Catherine Mead Street in every way except one. The feeling of unity, which was so obvious when we left Catherine Mead Street, was just as tangible here. The vital thread was the common cause which everyone was making against the Germans. But it took my brothers and me some time to be accepted by the local kids.

I now had another brother, David Howard. The name "David" was given to him simply because my mother liked it. The "Howard" part was the Christian name of the minister at Penn Street Tabernacle, for whom my father had enormous respect. (I would like to have shared his adulation; but how could you take a man seriously who could make a sermon last for over an hour?)

David was still a baby. He had been born in the disorder of the blitz and knew nothing else, although an extraordinary amount of attention was lavished upon him by us all because of the circumstances. But George and I were that much older; we were strangers in a strange land, and our new playmates were not intending to give us much time to establish our position in the order of things. Lynton Road was a tough area with a fearsome reputation. There was nothing cosy here as there was in Catherine Mead Street. There were no corner shops, no Mr Mayo to console us, or Frank Eddolls to provide our comics once a week or cut our hair once a month. The school and the shops and the buses were a considerable walk away. The locals already had their own gang, and they were not about to let us in easily. So far they were not exactly hostile, but they were certainly watching us very carefully, and our probation period was fast running out. If you didn't tread hard in Lynton Road you got trodden upon, and we learnt the lesson very quickly.

But Lynton Road had advantages which Catherine Mead Street could never match. Our new home was in a road built in lines of houses grouped in fours. No.97 was one of the two middle houses in a quartet, and a narrow covered passageway divided us from our

49

other central neighbour. Unlike Catherine Mead Street there was a small garden in front and a large one behind. Privet hedges, some neatly trimmed but most growing abundantly, paralleled the houses along the length of the road and divided them from each other from front gate to back. At the top of the garden was an Anderson Shelter, which we shared with one of our neighbours. This looked to me to be a much safer proposition in an air raid then our stair-cupboard in Catherine Mead Street. Thick corrugated iron sheets, curved inwards to meet at the top where they were bolted together, were sunk into the earth and packed hard with soil from the garden. It contained the usual wooden and flat wire bunks, and was entered from the front by a square opening in the steelwork, from which dropped a short wooden ladder.

The real joy of the house was the inside. There was a bathroom and a long deep bath. To use it you lit the copper boiler until the water was hot, and you pumped the water into the bath by operating a semi-rotary pump with a wooden handle. There was a cold tap at one end, and a plug to let it drain afterwards. There was also an inside toilet, although it was only just inside, in the porch by the back door. There was a kitchen and a living room, and a staircase, which led up to three bedrooms. At last George and I could sleep in separate beds. There was a big fireplace and plenty of cupboards and even a larder with a cold slab, which my mother, with recollections of all the years she had spent in service, looked upon with happy anticipation. Best of all, there was electricity. No more turning on the gas and fitting fragile silk-like mantles; one flick of the switch, and there was light everywhere (providing you had a shilling ready to feed into the meter). Very quickly we discovered other, more material, benefits of gas and electricity. When the men came from the Gas or Electricity Company to empty the meters every few months, they always left some coins on top of the square metal box. I never knew exactly why this was part of the accounting system, but those occasional little pile of pennies from the gas man, and shillings from the electricity man, meant that my mother could take us to the pictures, or out on a picnic, or to the Zoo; treats which could rarely be afforded in the normal way.

By now my father had left to join the army. He made no fuss. One day he just left us, and mother said he was off to Yeovil to join up, like all his family had done for years and years. Some people said he

50

should apply for exemption because of his age and the size of his family, but my father knew that would be cowardice of the worst kind, so off he went, and remained away for the best part of six years, confidently leaving my mother in charge of our upbringing.

What an extraordinary woman my mother was. She was no more than five feet tall, and rather dumpy. Her cornflower blue eyes reflected her every emotion. They sparked when she laughed, darted fire when she was cross, and quickly filled with tears when she was unhappy. Her hair was prematurely white, her complexion was ruddy, and when she smiled at you it made you feel that the world was a wonderful place to live in. Her temper was volatile. Although she was fiercely loyal and protective and loved us all dearly, she never let her devotion to us stand in the way of a good clout with her hand or with any weapon which came to hand. There was more than a touch of Irish in her, which accounted for her devout Roman Catholicism. She was never beaten. She would mend our shoes on a shoe-last when the "sixpences" began to appear in the leather soles. She had been a cook in service, and would make Sunday dinner last right through until Wednesday using the same ingredients cunningly treated. When we had no money she would make and sell toffee apples at the door. At Christmas-time she used to make dolls. I would paint the faces and stuff them, and we would sell them to neighbours. She took in mending and alterations to clothes, and had a job two or three times a week in Clifton as a charlady. She could play the piano and grow flowers, decorate the inside of the house and handled what little money we had from the family allowance my father sent from the army, with the care of a Swiss banker. She made jam and delicious cakes and pastries, and was never ill; or, more exactly, she never let us know that she was ill.

When she was a small girl she was taken from her home in the Bristol slums by her aunt, and sent to a convent near Porlock, in the care of French nuns. There she acquired a better-than-usual education for one of her background, and spoke fluent French, which she lost completely by the time she married my father. She was treated very harshly by the nuns, but learned to believe in God, and her faith never faltered. She could throw a ball as far as I could, cheated disgracefully when she played cricket with us, taught us to love books, and sat with me for hours helping me do my homework

51

when I went to Merrywood Grammar School. She was indomitable. She used to declare frequently that "there's no such word as 'can't' in the English language." She had moved around the country as a scullery-girl, maid, and cook, in some great houses in England, and she prized a Catholic prayer book given to her and lovingly inscribed by Lady Gainsborough. It was there, she told us in an unguarded moment, that she "walked out" with Cecil the footman. We pulled her leg about this, until she flew into a passion and picked up a cane, after which Cecil was never mentioned again. In spite of the dreadful drudgery, she always spoke kindly of the wealthy people for whom she worked. She sometimes went back down the years and told us about hunt balls, and the servants' quarters, and the good food they were given, and the pitiful wages of five or ten pounds a year, with scarcely any free time, and the uniforms they had to wear. She spoke of rutting stags on the estate, and the Christmas parties, and the magnificent napery and silver-ware which were produced for special occasions. She explained the rigid order of precedence among the serving staff, no less rigorous than that between the master and the servants themselves. The butler was supreme, followed by the housekeeper, the governess, the cook, the personal maids, down to the scullery maids, or "skivvies". Then there were footmen, and the array of outside staff, including the head gardener, the under-gardeners, the grooms, and the boys. Everyone knew his or her place, and a superior servant could be at least as cruel as an uncaring master to those below.

Her day began at dawn when she lit the fires and carried hot water to all the bedrooms. It ended in the dark, except for occasional days off. And all the washing and scrubbing and cleaning and polishing and waxing of floors was done on hands and knees; mechanical assistance wasn't available in those days. Always she was at the call of the bells when they jingled for immediate action.

She was found a place in service by her Aunt Charlotte, or Aunty Lottie as we knew her on the very rare occasions when she emerged from Cornwall. Lottie was housekeeper to a priest in a presbytery in Truro, and meant more than her own mother to my mother. She provided her with a tin trunk with the initials "A.K.H." inscribed on the top, my mother's maiden name being Annie Kathleen Hill. Into this trunk she packed all her belongings as she moved from post to post, and we kept it in the family for years.

My mother's father was a carter. He was killed, instantly and tragically, at Winterbourne, when the iron brake shoe holding the wagon flew free on the end of its chain. The heavy block described a swift, flying circle and brained my grandfather instantly. This left his widow to raise a son and two daughters with no money to do so; my grandmother must have been very relieved when my mother disappeared from the scene to earn her own living. One of my mother's prized possessions was a sepia picture of her great-grandfather. He had been the master of a sailing ship; his face was invisible under a profusion of whiskers, but he wore his peaked cap well, and I suppose it was from him that my mother derived much of her drive and determination.

So there we were, housed in a pre-war planner's dream of a council estate, my mother, three brothers, and a fourth one due. Father was in the army and we looked forward eagerly to his letters and his short leaves; meanwhile, we had to settle in and make ourselves comfortable. There was a school at one end of the estate, in Marksbury Road, and at the other end was Marksbury Road Library. To take care of our moral requirements there was Bedminster Road City Mission Church alongside the library, and St Hugh's, a prefabricated Church of England outpost in Lynton Road. Apparently shops and buses weren't necessary in the opinion of the planners, because it was at least a ten-minute walk to either. But, surmounting everything, and providing young boys with all they could ever need by way of adventure, was Novers Hill – "Up the Novers". It was, and still is, a huge natural grassy escarpment between Knowle West at the top, and Lynton Road at the bottom. All our houses had a back gate leading up the Novers by way of the allotments. There were hedges and bushes, and long grass to slide through like marauding Indians, and dens to be dug and covered over, and fires to be lit. In the summer, the Novers was often a mass of burning dead grass, and when the hedges caught fire as well it was a sight to behold.

If it snowed in the winter we had a huge, ready-made toboggan run. You could pick and eat sour-sobs, and blackberries, and, if you were dared, pee-the-beds. You could cut branches to make bows, and take strong, straight young suckers out of the privet hedges to make arrows. You could take a blob of mud, shape it into a ball, put it on the end of a pliable stick and hurl it for miles. You could cut

53

catapult forks out of the trees, fit it with rubber inner tube, add a pouch, and there was a catapult of frightening power, with which we became amazingly accurate.

There was also the "Stone Butt", as mysterious to us as the pyramids were when they were first discovered in the desert. It was a white concrete wall, with steps leading down in the ground at each end. Behind it, up the hill, no grass would grow and the surface consisted of permanently red soil. But when you dug into the earth there was always handfuls of spent bullets to be found. Obviously, it was built for rifle practice before the housing estate was constructed, in between the wars. The marksmen fired from a position where Lynton Road and Marksbury Road were now sited, at a target set in the red soil, with the scorers signalling hits or misses from behind the concrete wall. But the history of the thing didn't bother us much; what mattered was that here was yet another outlet for our imagination and enjoyment.

One day my brother and I found a huge iron rim of a cartwheel in the long grass. We stood it upright, pushed it downhill, and let it roll into the line of bushes below. It gathered speed, and to our horror it crashed unhindered through the hedge, gained speed across the allotments, and burst through a garden hedge. It bounced up and hit the back wall of the house precisely between two windows. If it had not hit the wall, its momentum would have carried it all the way to St John's Lane. We dare not even dream of the consequences. We fled into Knowle West and returned home by a circuitous route an hour later, trying to look innocent. Puzzlingly enough, we never heard this escapade ever mentioned. But it scared us to death.

Rivalling the Novers as a place of wonderment for us all was the Malago. As far as we were concerned it was a large stream that rose somewhere up on Dundry Hill, by Pigeonhouse Farm, and flowed down through Bishopsworth, through Locks Mills in Parson Street, to the 22 bus stop in Sheene Road where it disappeared down a culvert. On the way it regularly flooded all the land and houses between Marksbury Road and Parson Street to the delight of those of us who didn't live there.

At its angriest it would roar against the sides to the full height of the road bridge in Marksbury Road. At its most benign it would flow sweetly down from Dundry, changing its aspect every few hundred yards. In places it was deep enough to dam and pretend to swim in. Elsewhere, alongside Bluebell Woods for instance, its sides were steep and you could swing across it on a long rope suspended from a tall tree. And between Marksbury Road and Bedminster Road you could fish for sticklebacks, sand gudgeons, and redbreasts. And we all knew people who had caught trout in the Malago, although we never actually caught one ourselves.

A real Malago fisherman required a partner, a flattened-out sack, and a jam jar with string around the rim for carrying the catch home safely. Shoes and socks would be discarded, and you both got into the stream gripping the oblong sack by its two opposite ends. On the count of "three" you would trawl the sack gently against the flow along the bottom of the stream, until your arms were fully extended. Then you stooped to examine the contents. If there was a flash of silver, you had caught something, and you leaned over, prised it carefully from the sacking, and let it loose in the jam jar while you made the next trawl.

Nobody quite knew what to do with the fish once they had been captured. Like catching butterflies, the thrill was in the chase. We always said we would take them home and keep them, and feed them in a bucket of water. But by the time we had stopped to play football, or argue the point with an enemy, the poor fish had usually gasped their last, anyway, and were now floating belly-up in the jam jar. Necessity then usually gave way to virtue, and the corpses were fed to a suspicious cat, as though that was what we had meant to do all along.

11

The war had not forgotten us when it bombed us out of Catherine Mead Street; Hitler still had us very much in mind, and Good Friday 1941 was yet to come. The sirens wailed most nights in the same way as they did in Catherine Mead Street, but the drill was different. The occupants of the house next door apparently had declined to accept an Anderson shelter in their garden, but were delighted to share ours when the bombing became really serious. The son and the daughter were considerably older than we were, and were very kind to us. Jim was doing important war work and was not called up. He spent hours in our house, playing card games and table skittles to help us relax. His sister Grace was also very accommodating, but their mother was a dragon. George and I would spend as much of the day as we could spare in annoying the old lady because she constantly told us off for nothing. Yet at night we all walked our garden path together and did our best to be pleasant to each other while the bombs and the shells racketed away outside. She was concerned above all to make sure she had brought her knitting and her snuffbox.

My mother said we should try to be kind to the old lady; she had no husband, and Jim had been very good to us. George happened to remark that he was not surprised that the old witch had no husband, and received a solid left hook in the ear from my mother for his pains. So we went out of our way to be helpful. We carried her ashbin out for her days before the collections were due, and had to carry it back in again while she yelled at us. We waited for her to come home from shopping so that we could help her with her bags, but she didn't trust us and told us to mind our own business. We even tried to clip her privet hedges for her as a surprise, but got called away to play football before we'd finished, and she stormed in to see my mother and dragged her out to see the mess we had made of her lovely privets. Yet every night we were forced to sit alongside her, and smell the snuff, and the mothballs, and the camphorated oil, which was apparently the only thing that would keep her alive at night. She grumbled when she was awake and she snored when she was asleep, and when she was only half-asleep she would swig cough medicine and help herself to her private store of cakes and biscuits. Jim and Grace could only look on in silent apology, whilst my mother, dead against her natural inclinations, would smile and chatter away nonsensically in a vain attempt to keep a pleasant atmosphere.

Our neighbours on the other side had their own shelter, but they rarely used it. He was a lorry driver, and she was a pleasant enough woman with whom my mother attempted to be friendly. They had a pretty young daughter whom we scorned utterly, because we didn't like girls, and there was a strange old man who was her grandfather. He was short and built like a cottage loaf, with a round head on top of a larger round body. He had watery blue eyes and a white moustache, set in a shiny red face. The only clothes I ever saw him wear were a navy blue suit which would not meet around his waist. His waistcoat was snowbound with cigarette ash, and the buttons strained hugely to keep his stomach in.

He kept rabbits at the top of the garden, and offered me thru'pence a time if I would fill a sack with dandelions for them. That was easy; the Novers could produce anything, so for a time I was doing well in the rabbit food business. Then one day he called me to the small two-posted fence that separated the houses where the privets ended, and said I was doing so well collecting dandelions, that he had another idea. Would I like to pick up fag-ends so that he could make roll-ups? I trotted indoors to discuss the proposition with my mother, and her reaction was instantaneous and pyrotechnic. She rushed out and described the old man's life and parentage in great detail, and threatened him with extremes of torture if he ever made such a suggestion again. The lady next door came to see who was being murdered, and when she heard the facts she joined in and told the old man some home truths of her own, causing him to retreat to his room in disorder. All this was no doubt very good for the souls of both of them, but it ruined my rabbit food enterprise forever, and left me looking for other propositions. The old man and I didn't talk much after that, except for the day when I told him that I had seen a black rat in his chicken run. I hadn't really, but it was very interesting to watch him puffing about before the chicken-wire, scattering rat poison everywhere.

I was assigned to what was Victoria Park Junior Boys' School in St John's Lane, right opposite the dental clinic. It was there that I met the schoolmaster who had the greatest influence a teacher could possibly have on a young boy's life. His name was Mr R C Taylor, and I shall never forget him or cease to be grateful to his memory for the way he helped me mature and see school as a place to be enjoyed and not a building in which you did sums and spelling tests and rushed home from as quickly as possible. He was by no means soft; in fact he believed strongly in discipline, and was as good canesman as I have experienced anywhere. On this subject I speak from long experience.

He was tall and well made, with broad shoulders and a slight stoop. His face was long, his nose was beaky, and his eyes were large and fixed intently upon yours when he spoke, so that you knew he could see right into your mind and know what you were thinking. But his teaching methods were remarkable. He would be solemnly playing the piano for hymns at assembly, when suddenly he would stop and hold the chord.

"How many notes can you hear?" he would roar to the startled school. Nobody answered.

"I'm playing four notes," he would bellow, and strike them one by one, and then in harmony, on the piano keyboard. "That is what you call music! The combination of different notes to make a tune. Don't just listen to the melody – listen to the harmony as well. See how many notes you can hear."

And he would carry on playing as if nothing had happened. But although half the school might have gone home, sadly convinced that the Head was going insane, there were many of us who listened, and could see the point he was trying to make, and tried it for ourselves, thus awakening a love for music.

Once he stopped when we were in the middle of singing "He who would Valiant be".

"Who wrote that?" he thundered. Nobody knew.

"That comes from *Pilgrim's Progress*, by John Bunyan. Who was John Bunyan?" Again nobody knew.

"Get the book out of the library, and read it," he ordered. He then continued roaring the hymn at us. And some of us actually did go away and read about John Bunyan.

On another occasion he crashed into a lesson by another teacher, apologised abruptly to her for the interruption, and demanded to know why a train would not go up a hill. We were locked for ages in

58

discussion, and he kept prompting and urging us towards the answer, until we were all straining to be the first to discover the reason. The David Williams, quiet but clever and destined to be an officer in the R.A.F. said "force of gravity".

"Very good answer, Williams," beamed Mr Taylor, nodded to his astonished colleague, and left the room, leaving us all bewildered at this sudden brain storming exercise. But he was teaching us how to think.

He had his select group of special pupils. They were not teacher's pets; he showed no favouritism to anybody. But he felt instinctively that boys differed from each other, and saw it as his duty to bring the best out of all of his charges, who came from a great variety of backgrounds and had special aptitudes and needs which required to be satisfied. Indeed, although his job was to turn boys into some sort of scholars, you knew that if he felt it necessary he would teach carpentry or boiler-making or French polishing with equal gusto and with the same eccentricity. Every Friday afternoon, in the last period of the week, he would keep his "specials" behind. We were all given a little blue exercise book – the one smaller than that known to all Bristol schoolchildren at the time, with the distinctive map of the Bristol area on the front. In this smaller book we had to write a report on any subject, in exactly 100 words (99 or 101 would not do); and to complete it within half an hour. We groaned at the sheer unfairness of this. We were being kept behind whilst the rest had rushed home laughing for the weekend. But it did not take the brighter ones among us long to realise that we were being taught to write with precision and economy of words, and to do so under the pressure of a time constraint.

His staff responded to his leadership. Miss St Hill encouraged us to bring in any drawing or writing we had done at home, and simulated raptures of delight at what we submitted, although no doubt she had seen it all a thousand times before. It was Miss St Hill who broke down the barriers of boredom for us, and introduced us to the beauty of poetry.

"Slowly, silently, now, the moon," she read. "Walks the night in her silver shoon".

"What's 'shoon', Miss?"

"Poetic licence, Budd. The poet thinks 'shoon' sounds better than 'shoes', even though there is really no such word."

"What's 'poetic licence' Miss?" asked Maurice Marks, and she would patiently explain, until we all saw the imagery of the moon as a being in its own right, walking alone and casting her light everywhere. Those of us who didn't see it were those who didn't want to anyway, and would never enjoy poetry however well it was served up.

Mr Spear read to us twice a week. From him grew a love of *Treasure Island* and *Kidnapped* which never left me. He could make us actually hear Blind Pew's stick tapping on the frosty road in the moonlight, as he approached the Admiral Benbow. But he was also quite happy to administer three of the best on each hand if we misbehaved, and then revert casually to the treachery of Long John Silver as though nothing had happened to interrupt the flow of Stevenson's prose.

School games day for the top form was the last session on a Wednesday. Mr. Taylor supervised the activity, which, summer or winter, took place in Victoria Park. There was a sports cupboard at school, containing odd bats and balls, some cricket gloves that wound on around the thumbs, and one or two footballs. There were no goal posts for us to use, but there were four wooden bollards. All the gear was carried by a long crocodile of boys, eager to be playing, and not complaining in the slightest about the loads they bore. That came on the way back, when the games were over.

This was the cricket season, and we marched up to Victoria Park, waited for Mr. Taylor to find a strip of turf without too many holes in it, and we drove the stumps in with the handle-end of the bat. Then Mr. Taylor solemnly marched 22 yards in the other direction, and three more stumps were driven into the ground. There were no bails. If anyone attempted to use the face of the bat to hit the stumps into the ground, he was sent immediately back to school with a "message" for Mr.Spear to deal with him.

Maurice Marks and I loved cricket, and there were some other doughty players available, especially Terry Butcher, who was very large, and inevitably found himself keeping wicket (and in goal, when we played football.) We picked the team with the captains tossing for first choice of players. All the stars were gathered rapidly into one team or another. If there were any problems, or if any boys arrived late, we used the ploy we all resorted to at home. They went "Pudd'n and Beef". The latecomers would be asked to move away secretly and nominate which one of them would be "Pudd'n", and which one would be "Beef". When they had made up their minds they returned, and one of the captains would call, "Pudd'n" (or "Beef"). The possessor of the name called would join the captain of the team who had called him, and the other would be in the ranks of the opposition.

Mr. Taylor said that this method had been used for centuries in the west country. He said that our use of the word "cree" had an ancient tradition. If we were playing a vigorous game, and wanted a break, we crossed two fingers and said "cree." This automatically suspended you from the game, and you couldn't be touched until you were ready to start again. Mr. Taylor said the Saxons originated this idea. He said that if the tribes had been fighting a battle for some time, and the dead and injured were piling up and seriously interfering with the real business, a chief would call "cree". Immediately the fun would stop, and all the dead and wounded would be cleared away. When the battlefield was tidy again, the chiefs would agree, and resume the slaughter. "Cree," he said, was Old English for "cross". You also found it in the town of Crewkerne, at the edge of the Mendips, where it originally meant "the place of the Cross". Joseph of Aramathea was a Phoenician trader who took Jesus with him over the Mendips, and whenever they stopped, they erected a cross. At least, that is what Mr. Taylor told us, and I believed everything he said.

The afternoon was cloudy, and not at all cricket weather. But we were out of school, and that in itself was a major benefit. We gradually became aware of a sole spectator. He was an American soldier. As usual with American servicemen, he was beautifully dressed, with a dark brown tie poked into his shirt buttons, a light fawn shirt, and dark brown trousers which were immaculately creased, and wearing so many medals that he looked like a Christmas shop window. He had three chevrons the right way up, and three connecting them, upside down. He wore an impressive peaked hat, so that, were it not for the stripes, you would have taken him for a major-general at least.

In between overs, he trotted over to Mr. Taylor, who was umpiring at both ends.

"Excuse me, Sir," he said politely, "Is this a game of cricket I am watching?" Mr. Taylor, impressively polite himself, acknowledged that it was.

61

"Could I try my hand, Sir?" he asked, "I used to be pretty good at baseball back home."

I swear Mr. Taylor winced and staggered slightly at the word "baseball" when used in connection with the game of cricket. He quickly recovered, and told the boy who was batting to hand the bat over to the American gentleman. Then he threw me the ball. "You bowl, Budd," he said, his voice heavy with emotion.

The American held the bat in a peculiar way. It was as if he had stooped and picked an axe off the ground, and was resting it on his shoulder, knees bent. I was so intrigued, I bowled him a full toss. The bat flashed, and the ball disappeared into the trees, still rising. While the boys ran to retrieve it, Mr. Taylor lowered his huge frame over me. "Any more of that rubbish, Budd, and you can give the ball to Marks."

The remaining balls of the over bounced at least once, and even Wally Hammond would have been pushed to score runs after the ball had hit that tangled turf. The American was then given the ball, and I was put in to bat. Again, his preparations were weird. He raised his front leg, circled his forearms around twice, and suddenly launched the ball at me with a yell. It flew inches from my head, and Terry Butcher, behind the wicket, dived for dear life as the ball rocketed away out of sight.

Terry got up and began to run for the trees. Mr. Taylor called out, but Terry was gone. "I ain't 'avin' no more of that," said Terry. "He'll kill I next!" Mr. Taylor looked at me scornfully. "What do you think your bat is for, Budd?" he hissed. But the American had worked it all out his system, was as happy as a lamb, and tossed me five soppy balls that I didn't deign to look at. "Thank you, Sir," he called to Mr. Taylor, as he replaced his cap and strode jauntily away.

Mr. Taylor had suddenly tired of cricket, so we pulled up the stumps, gathered the kit, and marched back to school in silence. Mr. Taylor had his head bowed, and seemed to be talking to himself. The word I heard clearest and most frequently was "baseball!"

Apart from these weekly escapes into Victoria Park to play games, the main business of the school, under the dedicated leadership of Mr. Taylor, was education; not strictly academic, but rounded, so that we were encouraged to let our logic fly off in a tangent if Mr.

Taylor thought it was leading anywhere. He also reinforced the attention Miss St. Hill and Mr. Spear were giving to our grasp of English literature. Sometimes he would casually mention authors, and say enough about the books they wrote to whet the appetites of some of us to find out more. "French Revolution?" I can remember him saying. "They took the heads off aristocrats and royalty until it became a hobby, and old ladies sat under the guillotine and got spattered with blood. You should hear what Dickens has to say about it in *A Tale of Two Cities*, or Baroness Orczy in her 'Sir Percy Blakeney' stories." There it was; the seed was sown, and if it withered and died on the stem, he would try again. But try he always did to lift our thinking above bombs and the pavements of Bedminster.

I had two tickets for Marksbury Road library, and could sometimes persuade Miss Greengrass, the librarian, let me have an extra book, because I devoured them so quickly. Once I saw Bob Flower, in the reference section. He said he was learning how to take and develop his own photographs. I had no doubt he would master the topic in a few days, and move on to other things, but for me, books were first and foremost about the written word, and secondly about the plot. While Bob Flower was teaching himself photography, I was reading about similes, and metaphors, and adjectives and prepositions, and loving it. One day a lad in the library said to me "Have you ever read the books by Arthur Ransome?" I didn't know who the lad was, but he enthused about *Swallows and Amazons*, and before long I had read every single Ransome book, including his autobiography. Had long ago milked William Brown dry. I loved Richmal Crompton's characters, but I had some difficulty in identifying myself with the deeds of a boy of eleven, whose household included a cook and a maid, and a part-time gardener. Mr Taylor often asked what I was reading. "If you like that, you'll like this," he would sometimes say, and pull down a book from his own shelves for me to borrow. I don't think I realised even then how fortunate I was to fall into the hands of such a teacher as Reginald C. Taylor.

12

The bombing was becoming more frequent. Novers Hill had been straddled by a group of four or five explosions, and there was now a line of craters from Knowle West to the engineering works in Parson Street marking their trail. The grass triangle in Wedmore Vale, opposite Clancy's Farm, was dug up and underground shelters were constructed. Occasional gaps were appearing in the ranks of houses as bombs landed, and our nightly visit to our air-raid shelter was, again, a regular feature of life. Sometimes mother didn't even bother to herd us together and hurry us to our refuge at the top of the garden.

Such was the case when the Good Friday Blitz shattered Bristol. The memory of that nightmare is particularly poignant because of my mother's Catholic beliefs. Good Friday, she always told us, was the most important event bar Christmas in the Christian calendar. It was the day that Jesus was put upon the Cross, and at three o'clock on every Good Friday afternoon, the skies would surely cloud over as they did when the temple veils were rent asunder. Somehow my mother acquired some fish for this very special day. There was no thought of Easter Eggs, of course, but she made a tray of toffee instead, and broke it into chunks and, as usual, we were quite satisfied. My younger brothers, after all, were really too young to remember special treats like Easter Eggs.

We spent the evening in the usual way. We played our games, read our books, and drew our pictures, until it was time to go to bed. The next few hours will remain forever as the terrible memory of a night of torture to which no child should ever be subjected. The sirens routinely threw out their obscene warnings; and then the air raid began in earnest. It was now too late and too dangerous for my mother to risk her brood out into the garden and to safety. Instead, she pulled the big wooden table up against the wall and made us huddle under it, with herself on the outside to give us extra cover. The lights were out; the blackout curtain was drawn; but the room was lit up like a thunderstorm with the flash of explosions. The bombs literally screamed down, frightening (as they were meant to) the life out of those who shuddered below and waited to see if this would be the one that did for them. As each bomb hurtled earthwards we stooped in unison, and cuddled into each other, until the detonation indicated that we had escaped and were still alive; at least until the next stick of explosives followed and remorselessly sought us out.

All the time, anti-aircraft guns fired ceaselessly, yet their noise was not sufficient to drown the sound of ambulances, and the shouting of people in the street outside. The disturbances were made all the more horrible because we had no idea of what was happening beyond the pathetic wooden table which we hoped, but didn't really expect, would save us from disaster. The terror and confusion went far beyond what we had experienced in the brick shelter in Catherine Mead Street, or the crypt under St Paul's Church. There was no defiant singing; no feeling of unity and comradeship. We were utterly on our own, and frightened stiff with terror. We curled up under that table and waited for the worst, with a feeling of abject helplessness. Even my young brothers were too horrified to cry.

And all the time, my mother and I thought of our father. We worried for him, wherever he was; and we knew that he would be a thousand times more worried about us. He had left his own family out of loyalty to his King and Country as was his ethic. Now we were quite alone and the thought of our plight must have been devastating to him. Yet he must have been aware that my mother, with her unflagging drive and steadfast devotion to us all, would be the one person to see us safely through anything which might befall.

At last, after an age of terror, the noise abated, the bombing ceased, and the guns grew silent. Into the air, with the sweetness of a draught of cool water in the desert, rose the soothing, forgiving voice of the "All Clear". For the moment we could relax. The electricity was disconnected and the only water we had was what my mother had prudently saved in various pots and pans in the sink. We lit the fire to make some toast, and went out into the street. Already neighbours were standing in groups and sharing any scraps of information they had gathered. A land mine had dropped at the end of the road, and had severely damaged Lynton Road and Marksbury Road. Nobody had any news about what had happened across Bartlett's Bridge and West Street or British Road, so I knew what my first task would be. I already had my coat on when my mother looked at me with a question in her eyes. Off I set to British Road to see how Auntie Jessie, Gran, and my cousins had spent the night. And my Uncle Fred too, no doubt; although why one of them could not make the trip in our direction to see how a family of three young boys and a father in the army was managing, was a thought my mother never allowed to flourish.

That journey was quite shocking. I was only eight years old, and I was told roughly, several times, by well-meaning men to go home and keep out of it. But I pressed on. Dawlish Road, a short road leading down into Marksbury Road was badly damaged. The nearest of those explosions which had terrified us during the night, had missed our house by no more than fifty or sixty yards. Marksbury Road seemed to be one long crater, and the stench of gas and sewage was choking. Brown liquid ran in channels, and twisted pipes looked up at us like bundles of frozen snakes. Here and there I passed signs saying DANGER – UNEXPLODED BOMB. But there was nothing to indicate what you were supposed to do if one of those bombs went off as you went by.

I saw too, the raw edge of nerves which my father had so untypically displayed last time I had visited British Road after an air raid; that time he had held himself back from the brink of savaging an innocent motorist who had sent half a brick in his direction. This time, a group of men were arguing when one of them lost his temper, grabbed another, punched him to the ground, and started to kick him. The others pulled him away; the victim got up, his mouth full of blood, and carefully dusted down his trousers. Then he walked away, and the other trudged off in the other direction, not sure what it had been all about in the first place, with the victor looking more sheepish than triumphant.

As usual, British Road was intact, and my relations, although pleased to see me, were only slightly interested in the tales of the night that I had to tell, so I came away as quickly as I could, to resume, at the age of eight, my responsibilities as the man of the family.

The baker and the milkman had both called while I was away. They both had carts drawn by horses. The milkman was usually very early, and all we knew about him was that he poured the milk into my mother's jug by using a brass measure on the end of a handle, and dipped it into a stainless-steel can. The baker we saw every day. His cart had two high wheels, and smelt deliciously of fresh bread. He himself was short and skinny, with a pointed shiny nose, a pinched face, and small, black, sparrow-like eyes, which missed nothing. He carried his large wicker basket hooked over one arm, and walked very quickly. He wore a trilby and a waistcoat, and short jacket with an apron, which I once called a "pinafore", and earned a clout for my cheek. Most striking of all was his pair of black leather gaiters, up to his knees, worn whatever the weather. He rarely spoke, but knew what pleased us. He sometimes chose our house to pause and feed his animal from the nose-bag on the footboard. With luck, the horse would produce some cannon balls, but our delight was diminished when my mother insisted that we collected them in a bucket and shovel because they were good for the garden.

There were several bodies set up at the time to "do good" for the sons and daughters of servicemen. It was at one of these charity gatherings that I first met my best pal, Bob Flower. His dad was away somewhere, driving a tank, and he and I had been carefully prepared to go to a "tea-party" in Wills' Hall in Bedminster. We played some games, which we thought were too young even for an infants' school; then, with a flourish, we were introduced to the food. To be fair to all, I must say that the sight of plate after plate of buns and cakes and confections, and sandwiches with mysterious fillings, did much to cheer us up after the food we had become used to. We sat around a table, and I watched the boy opposite. A lady was telling him not to "reach across", but to take his food from the nearest plate. This suited me, because I was sitting right in front of a big currant cake, and I grabbed a slice at once. Immediately my wrist was tapped and I was told to start with the bread and butter and "work up" to the sweet things later. I was indignant, but before I could say a word, the boy opposite spoke up.

"That don't make sense. You can't eat what's in front of you, and the food on the other side at the same time. Stands to reasons, don't it?"

I looked at him in admiration. He was a kindred spirit. Between us we soon had the kind lady apologising, favouring us with the jammiest plates, and rushing away in a torrent of tears before the end. I soon found out that Bob could speak grammatical English as well as anybody, but preferred to annoy people by talking

67

"Be'minster". He lived at "Thirty-three, Hall Street" but delighted in telling people like teachers and vicars that his house was "Fir'y-free 'All Street, Be'minster". By the railway line; thees know!" His junior school was Parson Street and when it was bombed he was placed in the senior school at Marksbury Road where he rose on merit to the second-top form before he was eleven years old.

Another charity venture which involved us was the giving away of toys and books by the Soldiers, Sailors and Air Force Association – S.S.A.A.F.A. I'm sure the group worked hard and did a lot of good in Bristol. But I found it humiliating to stand in line and be given the choice of some other child's second-hand belongings. Bob said he didn't mind a bit, as long as it was free; but I couldn't look at it that way. I didn't regard myself as one of the deserving poor. In the event, I chose two books, which I valued for years. One was a good, well-illustrated version of the story of King Arthur and the Knights of the Round Table. The other was called *Mutiny* by Charles Nordhoff and James Norman Hall. I remember *Mutiny* in particular. It was a well-researched account of the mutiny on H.M.S. *Bounty*, against Captain Bligh, and led by Fletcher Christian. On the flyleaf of the book was a note scribbled in pencil by the man who had bought it and given it to a friend. He said he had met Charles Nordhoff on a cruise recently and found him to be very interesting.

Another group set up at the beginning of the war, to help ease the strain on families with their men-folk away in the services, arranged for people to spend a week or two at Hinnegar Camp as a respite from the bombing. Hinnegar was the village next to Badminton, the home of the Duke of Beaufort. We were not the only guests of His Grace. Also in residence, and well away from the London Blitz, was the formidable Queen Mary, the Queen Mother. She was the widow of George V, the former Princess Mary of Teck, born when the aristocracy of the whole of Europe was linked with Queen Victoria and her progeny.

We had a marvellous two weeks in the tents at Hinnegar. There were woods and streams, and trees to climb, and hidden paths and secret dens. There was also some organised entertainment, which we skilfully avoided because we were too busy enjoying ourselves.

The estate workers were very old men; forty at least, and we used to watch them trimming the trees and burning the wood in gloriously satisfying bonfires. They used axes and reap-hooks, and

68

we helped them drag away the branches and heave them into the roaring flames until our faces were black and our hair was singed and freckled with wood-ash. It was during one of these blissful burn-ups that the grand old lady appeared. She stepped out of a large shiny black car, waited on by two men in trilbies who seemed unable to bow low enough. Although she was incredibly ancient, she was as straight as a lamp-post. She was dressed in blue; her hat was like a silk flowerpot, and she wore a veil, sprinkled with blackcurrants, partially obscuring her eyes. She had an orange hue from too much make-up, and her dress swept right down to her ankles. She was carrying a flimsy sort of umbrella, which I thought would be useless if it came on to rain; but she was using it to point at my companions and me.

The two men seemed angry. They called us over and shouted, "What have you done with the bill-hook?" As youngsters from Bedminster we had no idea what a bill-hook was, and we said so. They wouldn't even listen to us. "You've stolen a bill-hook from the workers," shouted one, seemingly looking at me in particular. He gave me a loud dressing-down and returned to the old lady, who shook her head sorrowfully and was driven away.

Back at the campsite, the officials already had us marked down as the boys who stole the bill-hook, and I was the ringleader of a gang of grand larcenists. In spite of my mother's indignant objections, they searched our tent thoroughly but of course they found nothing. My sense of fair play had been offended, and I bitterly resented being called a thief in front of everybody, when I knew that I had done nothing wrong.

Several days later there was enormous excitement. Queen Mary was due to pay the camp an official visit, and we were all scrubbed and polished until we were deemed hygienic enough to meet her majesty. The huge car rolled up, and out stepped the regal old lady with the useless umbrella. The organisers introduced her, we all clapped as we had been instructed, and the man who had accused me of thieving produced a big red tin. Soon the Queen Mother was handing out toffees, one each, as we queued to receive our gift and tried to summon up the courage to look this Important Person directly in the face. When my turn came, I refused, but my mother gave me a persuasive clip in the ear, so I took the toffee, and glared at the man. The Queen Mother may possibly have recognised me, because she turned her head stiffly and whispered something to the man, the practised smile never leaving her face. The man promptly patted my head, dipped into his pocket, and produced a shilling. "We found the bill-hook in the hedge," he beamed, and turned at once to the next supplicant in the queue.

"Did you!" I said to myself, filling with rage; and turned and fled headlong into the woods. I wanted to be on my own. The man had named me to everybody as a thief and hadn't even said he was sorry. I was still clutching the toffee and the coin. "They can keep their sweets, and their money," I yelled, and flung both as far as I could into the undergrowth.

Strangely my mother wasn't cross when I returned; she didn't even ask me where I'd been. She just waited for me to say something. "I don't want their stuff," I said defiantly, and looked anxiously up at her. She didn't want an explanation, really. I reckon she knew exactly how I felt. "Come and get ready for bed," was all she said. But I knew she wasn't a bit angry. In fact, although she never said so, I think she was quite pleased with me.

13

The blitz had terrified its victims, but the thought of what might follow worried everybody, particularly parents. Nobody knew how long it would last, or how long it was advisable to continue the risk of losing young lives without taking some preventative action. People were still as defiant and unyielding as ever, but our armed forces did not seem to be doing very well. All letters home from servicemen were heavily censored, but too many people had relatives doing the actual fighting for everything to be kept totally secret. There was no jauntiness discernible now; just a determination to plough on to the end, whatever that might be. What worried parents most was the well-being of their children. We knew of kids at school whose families had moved right out of Bristol altogether, and others who had gone a shorter distance as far as Clevedon or Weston-super-Mare.

The government decided that the choice of evacuation from the endangered cities into the countryside should be available to everybody. My mother, no doubt after writing to my father about the matter, decided that my brother George and I would be evacuated, which would leave her looking after David and baby Philip. George and I were told, rather than consulted, about the move, and we broke our hearts to think that we were due to be shipped out of Lynton Road to an unknown place many miles away from our family and our friends.

So it was that, one morning in May 1941, George and I stood outside Marksbury Road School, with dozens of other children, waiting for the coaches to take us to Temple Meads railway station and on to somewhere into Cornwall, wherever that was. The mothers were there to see us off, and there was much wailing and sobbing, and hugging and kissing, often to the astonishment and suspicion of some lads who had never been cuddled by their parents in their entire young lives. Slung over our shoulders on lengths of string were our cardboard boxes containing our gas masks, and we carried our clothes in small cases or brown paper carrier bags with string handles. The boys wore caps and ties, and grey socks, kept up by elastic garters. If we possessed a raincoat, we wore that too, tightly buckled about the waist. We had luggage labels attached to our coat collars so that we could be identified in case anything happened. In particular we had envelopes, stamped and addressed to our mothers, with strict orders to write as soon as we arrived. Most of us had little parcels of cakes or sandwiches for the journey; but these disappeared long before we boarded the train.

Several teachers were in charge of the party, and they were kept fully occupied early in the journey. Travelling by train was a new experience except for Sunday School outings to Weston, and there was much to do. We rushed up and down the corridors and into other compartments, to greet old friends and renew battles with old enemies. We gazed in wonderment at the scenery as it unravelled before us, and saw miles and miles of green fields, and hills in the background, and cows, and wheeling birds, the like of which we had never come across before. But the novelty soon began to melt, and we tried to scrounge food from those who had been more prudent than the rest, and still had some left. The windows had to be kept closed, said the teachers, to keep out the ashes, which could blind you in an instant; and the train rocked and clattered onwards unendingly until we were mesmerised by its rhythm. Then we mostly sat and talked, or dozed; I clearly recall one of the older boys asking a teacher "How far to our destination, sir?" and realising that I was quite ignorant of what the word "destination" meant. I asked the boy and he sneered and told me to ask the teacher myself. Luckily the teacher overheard all this, and told me that we were still several hours away from where we were going, and I had to be satisfied with that.

None of the railway stations had place names showing. They had been removed in case the Germans suddenly arrived, and discovered where they were from road signs and names on railway platforms. I thought once again how foolish the Germans must be, if they couldn't work out where they were. After several hours we came to a huge grey bridge over muddy water, and the word soon got around that this was Plymouth. That bridge would have provided a clue to their whereabouts to even the dullest Germans, and we knew that we were now crossing the Tamar into Cornwall.

On we went, hungry and growing ever more tired and anxious. The thrill of the journey had long since vanished and we were now worrying where we would be sleeping that night, and who would be looking after us tomorrow and in the future. Some of us were already homesick.

The train made one or two stops, and then it was our turn. We climbed out onto a platform, into the dusk at a place called Truro. For all we knew it could have been anywhere in the world, and by this time we didn't much care. But our journey was far from over. We clambered into a bus and were soon rumbling deep into the countryside. It was dark by the time we reached a large country house on the Truro to Redruth road. The coach turned into the drive and we decanted and were ushered in through some huge doors to a large hallway. A bossy lady took the list of evacuees from the last remaining teacher, checked it, and signed it as being correct. We were all there, and ready to spend our first night in Cornwall. But it was here that the system stopped working. The bossy lady was assisted by a nervous young woman who fluttered about us like a butterfly. She was obviously acutely aware of her responsibilities and wanted to do her best for us. Unfortunately she was frightened to death of the older woman, and severely hampered by the fact that there was no food on the premises. In tears she pointed this out, but the bossy woman, who no doubt had been taking three meals a day up to that point, was quite unmoved. In Churchillian tones, she described the lack of supper as of nought when compared to our unending fight against Nazi domination. We kids weren't feeling particularly patriotic. We thought ruefully of the feast we had made of our food while the train was still warming up in Temple Meads station. She said she thought she could manage a cup of tea and a slice of bread for each of us, to see us through until the morning. This brought squeals of dismay from the kind young lady, and didn't really help much. It only underlined our unfortunate plight.

At last we were given a snug little bed each, and I tried to say my prayers without anyone noticing. I think George did the same. We all said them together, every night, at home, kneeling at the side of the bed; and we were in severe trouble if we tried to skip any of the words or say it too quickly.

We had been taught to say:

God bless Daddy and Mummy;
God bless John and George;
God bless David and Philip, and make us good boys.

73

And please God, keep us safe from all harm and danger.
And bless all those who are suffering tonight. Amen.

But that night I found those words difficult to say, even to myself.
My pillow was damp with tears, and my nose seemed to be leaking.
I thought of my mother, alone in Bristol with my two baby brothers,
and my father, at a place unknown to any of us, helping to fight this
war.

Next morning, somebody had already arrived with supplies. The
helpful young lady had stopped depressing us with her snivelling,
and we waded in to a solid breakfast of cereals, milk, toast, beans,
and plenty of hot tea. Our guardians seemed to think that hot tea
was some kind of magic cure-all for kids from the city; pour a cup
down our throats and we would function untended for ages, like a
well oiled engine.

We gathered our belongings and packed them back into our
cases; and the big moment had come. Now was the time when we
were to meet our replacement parents for the first time. George and
I stood alongside each other and examined the prospects uneasily as
our hosts surrounded us and made all sorts of critical remarks about
us. They did actually stop short of peering at our teeth and feeling
our muscles, but only just. I suppose we should have felt grateful
to these people who had offered to look after us for the duration of
the war. But we hadn't exactly asked to come; all of us, given the
chance, would have opted to stay home and take our chance
alongside our families. But I expect they thought they were being as
patriotic as my father, when they volunteered to share their homes
with strange children from the big city. And I couldn't suppress the
thought that whoever picked Bisto Smith was in for a shock when
the patriotism wore off.

At last George and I were accepted as a pair by a lady whose
glasses caused her to blink uncertainly, as if she had not yet come to
grips with the world. She didn't say much; she never did. Husband
Walter and son Wally were very much in charge. Her hair was
turning grey and was straight and cut very short, with no attempt at
style. She carried a shopping bag permanently over one arm, and
walked with a slight stoop. That, and her bad feet, made her look
frail, although she was far from ancient even by our standards. She
went out each morning and returned at tea time and I never, ever

74

knew what she did, where she went, or even what her Christian name was. She signed for us and we all went off together in silence. We never knew any more about her than what we saw on that blustery May morning as we walked down the hill to her cottage.

The air was warm and damp, and the landscape was something we had never experienced before. The house was in a line of half-a-dozen, just out of the village of St Day. Twenty years previously the tin mines here had petered out or grown too dangerous or too uneconomic to work. In all directions there were ruined pumping houses with their gaunt, tall chimneys. There were limitless piles of rubble, which were called barrows. There were mine shafts, most of them protected by circles of tumbledown stone walling. Sometimes these shafts were overgrown and concealed by wreaths of brambles and hedges of stinging nettles. Later we would learn to throw a rock down the neck of a shaft and wait long, thrilling seconds until we heard it splash into the water far below, emitting satisfying clangs as it ricocheted from side to side on its flight downwards into the void. There was a pond up in the abandoned workings, and it provided water for the hamlet and a home for a million frogs and tadpoles. The surrounding rubble was iron coloured, and the little rivulets which ran through it were the colour of rusty nails. In places, a track wound its way through the barrows, and occasional wooden sleepers marked the base of a small-gauge railway system which took the effluent from the pits and dumped it on the barrows. There were upturned, rusting iron trucks, whose wheels could still be spinning gently if you thought hard enough; and there were the shells of granite stone buildings with no doors nor window frames, or even roofs. If you put your head under a ruined chimney stack and looked up, you could see a fluorescent green coating glowing brightly at the top. This, we discovered, was called "verdigris" formed over many years by the constant reaction of chemical-laden smoke on the granite masonry. The whole area was silent and mysterious. A couple of goats were tethered behind the cottages, although little grass seemed to grow in the tightly compressed earth. Trees waved in the distance; the solid square shape of a Methodist chapel rose over a hedge, and old, cob-walled cottages, some of them thatched, stood randomly, and brooded silently, alongside the road to Truro. We turned into one of the front gates and up a short strip of concrete path to the front door of our new home in Cornwall.

14

Young Wally hadn't gone to school that day; the arrival of the evacuees from Bristol was far too precious an occasion to miss. He was a year or two older than me, and slightly larger, and his appearance made me wonder how he would fare at the hands of Bisto Smith and some of the more violent young gentlemen in Lynton Road. He wore a ring on one hand, and George and I had never in our whole lives seen a boy wearing a ring. He was clean and tidy, and his golden hair sported one or two fetching waves, which must have taken his mother a long time to cultivate. He smiled at us, and even his teeth seemed a little too perfect. His mother was obviously very proud of him, and there was no doubt that he was well used to being admired. Still, he seemed pleasant enough. He said nothing out of place, but always there was a feeling of unease, and the thought that we were yet to see another side of young Wally.

At teatime, after Wally had taken us up into the mine workings and showed us how to throw stones down the shafts, we sat in the kitchen and waited for the return from work of Mr Wally. What his work was, we never found out, but we reckoned he must have been a miner or employed by one or other of the active tin mines around St Day. He had no car, and I don't recall ever seeing him ride a bike. He went out early and came home regularly at about five o'clock. What he did in between, we were apparently not required to know. Certainly Mrs Wally and Wally were permanently in awe of him. That evening we sat nervously and waited for him to appear.

It was rather like the entry of the wicked baron in the pantomime. The back gate clanged, the kitchen door opened, and there stood Mr Wally, peering at us. He was short and pear-shaped. His hair was black and curly, his complexion was dark, like a gypsy's, and his eyes, beneath his low black eyebrows, floated in yellow tears. They were brown and penetrating, and he studied us with the intensity of someone who needed to look very hard before he understood. His mouth was set in a permanent leer, and his teeth, with prominent gold fillings, were slightly bared through parted lips. He shook hands with both of us, and sat down at once to the plate of food, which the well-trained Mrs Wally had already brought in at a trot from the scullery. We watched, fascinated, while he consumed his dinner at an astonishing rate. Then he accepted a mug of tea, sipped it, blew into it, and looked at us again.

"Where does your father work?" he asked.

"He's in the army," I said, realising as I spoke that my eyes suddenly began to sting at this reference to my father.

"What did he do before that?" I told him that he swept the roads and was also a dustman. He sneered as he reached again for his tea. "He must have arms like a bull," he said. He seemed pleased with his expression, and he repeated it. "He must have arms like a bull."

I was shocked into silence. Why on earth did he have to say that? For me, that was the end of Mr Wally. My father had worked hard, praised his Maker, cared for a growing family, and left them to fight for the country because that was what his principles told him to do. And here he was, being dismissed in one bizarre sentence by a man who knew nothing about him, as having "arms like a bull". I never forgot that.

There was no electricity and the light came from a large lamp on the table. Nobody spoke very much. Wally's parents, beyond sketching out the arrangements for school next day, asked very few other questions. We had cocoa and some biscuits and went to bed. I read by the light of the diminishing dusk until it was too dark to see the pages. George and I were sharing a room and a bed, in the front of the house, and our view swept across the barrows and the fields, up the hill to the road to Truro. Very occasionally, vehicles went by. Petrol was rationed and few people possessed cars anyway. I stood at the window in my familiar pyjamas and watched the infrequent traffic. I began to feel very lonely. I prayed that one of these motors might contain the bossy lady; and she might stop at the cottage, and say it had all been a mistake, and she would whisk us on to Redruth and put us on the train to Bristol and back to the security of my capable, comforting mother. But dusk turned into darkness and I climbed into bed beside my brother and pulled the sheet around my ears, whispered my prayers, and went to sleep.

Next day, we went to school. It was a short walk up the hill to the village of St Day. We passed a few shops and a chapel, and, just as the road narrowed to a track, we were at the school gates. There was a playground and the aura of the school was very much like that of Victoria Park junior school, with its outside brick-built toilets and its assembly hall, its glass-windowed classrooms, and its high ceilings. The children were rushing around the playground waiting for the whistle to go into assembly, and I thought that in this respect at least, St Day was no different from Bedminster. There were several evacuees already attending the school, but they were mostly from London. There was certainly nobody there that we knew. The teacher was friendly enough as he registered us in, but the local children were inquisitive, and very anxious to see what George and I looked like. Mrs Wally had equipped us with the standard lunch for Cornish village schoolchildren; a pasty and a bottle of cold tea. We had doubts about this at first, but before several weeks had passed we quite enjoyed it.

It took us some time to fit into this new school. We had problems with the language at first, or at least with the dialect. It was much like Bristol, for example in the way they rolled their "R's". But the burr was exaggerated, and it took us ages to start referring to girls as "maids", and saying "me 'andsome" to a pal, and to refer to the big farmers as "maister" and to interpret a dozen other peculiar nuances of speech.

We also noticed at once that, whilst most of the children dressed quite normally, there were those who were obviously desperately poor. Some wore wooden clogs, and one or two had no shoes at all. The teachers seemed to treat the unfortunate ones with extra care and sympathy; but the pupils were as bitterly cruel as only children know how to be, and poked fun at them for their poverty. There was a fair amount of fighting outside of the gate after school, and the destitute children, who were obviously accustomed to a regular battering, often had the best of things, no doubt because they had done it so often. The fighting was scrupulously fair. The others formed a circle, coats were removed, and if one got knocked down he was allowed to get up and nobody touched him while he was on the floor. What I found odd, particularly with recent battles in Lynton Road very fresh in my mind, was that if one of the combatants said he had had enough, he was allowed to put his coat on and walk away. To do that in Lynton Road would amount to signing your death warrant. Perceived cowards were despised more than bullies, unfortunately.

George was too small to bother anyone, but I had several tussles quite quickly. This didn't bother me because I knew that, sooner or later, somebody would be sure to try me out on behalf of the locals, and if I didn't make my point at once, I would suffer for it later. On one occasion they arranged that I would fight one of the very poorest boys, and when I walked out of the school gate I entered a ring of excited, yelling youngsters and saw this poor lad looking sadly at me. He held his young sister by the hand. Her dress was in tatters, her eyes were too big for her face, and she was snivelling and wiping her nose on her wrist. She had no shoes and he wore a pair of wooden clogs, fringed with brass rivets, and slightly pointed at the ends. He looked at me with an empty face and then, with an awful air of resignation, let his sister's hand drop. She folded her elbows across her chest, clutched her hands to her shoulders, and looked at her brother with desperate anxiety. Without any expression on his face, he moved towards me, his clogs making a clopping sound on the roadway. I had never been so deeply sorry for anybody in the whole of my young life. I felt like crying and hugging him, and walking him back to his sister and seeing them safely away. I wasn't in the least bit afraid of him. I just felt that the whole thing was wrong. It was utterly unfair and should never be happening. So I did something which, on reflection, I considered to be very mature. I stood where I was and said that I would not fight this lad on any account, but since we were all gathered together and expecting some entertainment, I would have a go at anyone else who felt he would like to take his place. Or words to that effect. Nobody offered, and the boy and his sister, with much dignity, walked off, hand in hand. I can't claim that he ever thanked me, or that I even spoke to either of them after that. But one or two of the bigger boys told everyone to go home, and they all quietly drifted away. George and I walked back to Mrs Wally's (strange that there was no sign of Wally during the affair), and that was the end of the matter. I had made a big impression on the schoolchildren without having to fight, and, not only that, I felt very warm inside.

There were a couple of young Catholic boys called Moss among the London evacuees. One was my age, and one was older, and from time to time they were whisked out of class to attend Mass on a holy day in the Catholic calendar. Naturally this did not surprise me, in view of my mother's religious proclivities, but the reaction of the local people (Methodist to a man) to Roman Catholics was frightening. They were genuinely held to be un-Christian and in need of regular chastisement. The two Moss boys suffered unending persecution from the rest, and it was no surprise to us when they went back home to London.

Another thing I noticed was the fact that some of the older women had swollen necks, bags of ugly flesh which hung from under their jaws. I asked about this and was told that these women suffered from goitres, brought about by the mineral in the water. Many houses were not connected to mains water; Wally's house was plugged into the pool on the hill, among the tips and barrows. A water cart went regularly around the village dispensing water to those who had no supply whatsoever, while others used springs or wells for all their needs. Sometimes, when the tap just above the skirting board in Wally's kitchen was turned on, it ejected dead tadpoles, but nobody except George and me seemed in the least bit surprised. We were quite startled. Even Catherine Mead Street had mains water.

Unlike in Bristol, the fish-and-chip shop opened at about five in the afternoon. At home, fish and chip shops never opened before seven, in time for supper. Here there was only one chip shop in the village, and a queue regularly formed at teatime.

Customers came from miles around. In Bedminster we had to walk everywhere, but here, once you left the fringe of the village, there was absolutely nothing except empty road until you reached another hamlet, usually miles away, like Chacewater, or Scorrier or Carharrack, and even smaller than St Day. Some people kept ponies, not only for pleasure, but because they were the only form of transport. Even fewer, usually farmers, had what they called "jingles". They were small carriages with high wheels, drawn by a single pony, and sufficient to carry a driver and passenger, and some light baggage or a couple of milk churns to and from the village or even to Redruth or Truro. The farmers were excellent drivers, and they rattled along the narrow lanes, giving the pony every encouragement by the snap of a long, thin whip, and by making strange noises, which the beasts seemed to understand.

There was a Methodist Chapel in St Day, but a more famous one a mile or so outside of the village, at Gwennap. Alongside it was a deep, grassy hole in the ground, obviously the site of a collapsed mine working. The Cornish people are highly superstitious, and stories which surrounded Gwennap Pit were legendary. The Wesley brothers, John and Charles, had preached there many times to desperately impoverished tin miners, who gathered down the slopes of the bowl to listen to the preachers on a rough-and-ready pulpit below. I could never believe that thousands of people could enter this hole in the ground at the same time, but the locals said they did, and hundreds were converted to Christianity.

And so May rolled on into June, and then July, in that tiny terraced house in the huge, scarred area of the otherwise beautiful Cornish countryside. But there was no love to be had in Wally's house. There was basic care, like food and a good bed, but not the slightest feeling of affection. Never did George or I feel the urge to give Mrs Wally a grateful hug or even a kiss, which might have been natural. Certainly she never hugged us. She remained as she was when we had first met her; silent and inscrutable, her eyes behind her glasses blinking at the perplexities of the world, her mind perpetually occupied elsewhere. She loved Wally, obeyed Mr Wally blindly, and that seemed to consume her complete stock of tender feeling. Mr Wally shoved us, occasionally snarled at us, but never actually hit us. He could bully us in other, more lasting, ways.

He used to make us go with him on walks over the barrows. He frequently stooped and picked up a lump of rock, examined it and threw it away without comment. This was what made us think he had something to do with tin mining. George and I used to speculate that he was trying to find a lost silver mine and get rich overnight. One Sunday evening, during one of these hikes, I walked with him up the hill to St Day, and I tried to show him a bird's nest I had found in a hole between the granite rocks of a wall. I loved roaming the area alone, and I had noticed that a bird was making frequent visits to this wall, always with its beak loaded. I looked in and saw half a dozen tiny beaks waving at me and squeaking loudly. I showed Mr Wally the spot. He clambered across the small ditch and looked in.

"Chicks," he said, and scooped two fingers into the gap, so that the tiny bits of flesh fell out of their nest onto the floor, and perished at once. He looked at me, and leered out of his dark face, and we walked on. I hated him for that.

It was also my task, when I came home from school, to take the wicker basket with the long, looped handle, which was left outside the locked door for my benefit, and fill it with half-grown black-berries before I was allowed in. I don't know what Mrs Wally used them for. One afternoon, Wally came to supervise me. He didn't help, of course; he watched, and jeered at me, and told me to hurry up or he would tell his dad. Nearby a goat was tethered, and Wally said I ought to practise milking it, because when his mother didn't need any more blackberries she would want some goat's milk. I had never seen a goat before, and looked with suspicion at this odd creature, with its dangerous-looking horns, its projecting beard, and its rotating lower jaw. Wally showed me where to start, and I bent down and grabbed a firm handful of what I was assured were its teats. As directed, I gave a good squeeze, and a sharp downward tug. The goat went wild, screamed, and hurled itself at me to the limit of its chain tether. When it found it couldn't reach me it kicked up its heels and brayed, and tried to charge at me, time and again, always being restrained by its leash. In its frenzy, it knocked over the basket of skinny green blackberries, which I had taken so long to collect. Risking my life, as I thought, I retrieved the basket, collected as much of the fruit as I could, and raced home. Wally was there already, and was joyfully telling his father how I had tried to milk the Billy-goat out on the barrows. For the first time, I saw Mr Wally laugh.

George and I got very depressed. Wally wasn't quite sure if he could take me on, but he had no fear of my small brother, and teased him ceaselessly. He was sly; a good punch was beyond him, because he might get caught. He went in for digs and pinches which Mrs Wally would never see, and which his father would ignore even if he knew. He loved to make cruel remarks about my family, and would point out how lucky we were to be with him, because our family could be killed at any time in the blitz. One evening, in the gloom of our bedroom, George and I concocted a letter to my mother. We told her we were bitterly unhappy, and we pleaded to be brought home. Foolishly, we asked Mrs Wally to post it. I don't know if it was ever sent, but it certainly provoked no response from my mother, which in itself was very unusual.

Then we heard that our Auntie Lottie was about to pay us a visit from the Presbytery in Truro, where she was housekeeper to the parish priest. We knew that my mother revered Auntie Lottie, in reality her Aunt Charlotte, but we could not remember seeing her before. She came on the bus from Truro, and we met this fine looking, white-haired old lady for the first time. She was dressed all in black, and her hat had a black veil. She was utterly calm and dignified in all that she did, and soon had Mrs Wally in awe of her. Tea was made and handed out in china cups which we had never seen before. Auntie Lottie sat as stiff as a ramrod, took her cup delicately between finger and thumb, and sipped the contents as though she took tea daily with the King. I half expected Mrs Wally to bob and curtsey; and Wally was either silent or missing. I can't say that we warmed to Auntie Lottie particularly; she was too distant, and a shade lofty, so we didn't feel comfortable. But she did represent our mother, and to that extent she was very welcome indeed. She asked many questions, thanked Mrs Wally most kindly, gave her some money for us (which pleased us), and for Wally (which didn't). She caught the bus back to Truro and Wally couldn't wait to tell his dad about this funny, posh old lady, who had come from Truro to see us. Mr Wally's response was what we might have expected. He rolled the words "Auntie Lottie" around his tongue in several different impressions of our aunt, each one more hurtful than the last. All the time his wet grin widened in his gypsy face, and we hated him all the more.

George just didn't fit in, and I never understood why. He was not naughty, and didn't misbehave more than any other young child of six would do in the same circumstances. But one day a car arrived and a fussy, officious lady got out. She said that George had to go to a hostel in Perranporth, but that I could stay. She gave no reason, but Mrs Wally was obviously expecting the visit, because George's little bag, packed and waiting, was produced from the front room where it had been concealed. George yelled, and clutched at the furniture, so that it took two grown-ups to dislodge him and hustle him into the car, assisted all the way by the gleefully dancing Wally. I didn't know what to do. In fact, there was nothing I could do except watch my young brother, looking out of the car window with his face streaming with tears, being driven away by strangers to a place I had never heard of.

The same afternoon, to console me, I suppose, they took me by bus to the seaside, and for the first time I saw how different was the roar of Atlantic rollers, and the mighty sucking of the shingle, from the tired muddy rippling of the Bristol Channel at Weston-super-Mare. But I was too upset and apprehensive to take much notice, wondering all the time whether I would be the next to go.

Next afternoon, Wally became very bold and tried to hit me. I can't remember what the disagreement was about, but it resulted in him chasing me over the barrows and threatening all sorts of retribution when he caught me. This was most unlike Wally. He usually waged underground warfare, and then almost exclusively with my brother who couldn't hit back, and when his father was there to protect him. I wondered what had made him confident enough to start bullying me openly. He was bigger than me, but not particularly pugilistic, merely a sneak. I was never afraid of him, and I guessed that the time had come for me to tell Wally what our relationship would be, now that they had caused my brother to be sent away in misery.

I stopped suddenly, and picked up a rock. "Wally," I said, "If you don't leave me alone from now on, I'm going to hurt you, and keep hurting you until you have had enough."

He eyed the rock but didn't believe I would use it. Already his newly found courage was seeping away like sand out of a sand bag. "I mean it," I said, and swung the rock at him. It caught him in the lower ribs and all the air shot out of his lungs in one gasp. He clutched his side, and sat on the ground, and began to cry. "You'll get that every time you touch me,"I said ferociously. "And sometimes you'll get it when you don't expect it. And if you run home and tell your Mum and Dad, I'll give you another one tomorrow when you're not looking. So go away and leave me along." Bisto Smith would have been proud of me.

I walked away, and I noticed that Wally wandered around a little, no doubt waiting for his eyes to dry. Then he went home, and when I followed it was apparent that Wally had kept quiet about the encounter because his parents didn't say a word. I had no trouble with Wally after that.

15

I was becoming very friendly with the boys from the Prophet family. Mr Prophet farmed his one-man holding on some land which straddled the road into St Day and quite close to the barrows. Gerald was the eldest, very big and strong, who didn't bother with school but spent much of his time helping his father. Dennis was the next in age. He was my hero, and his mind was never still. He was lean and active, and seemed always to have finished what was to be done before the rest of us had even identified the problem. He built a floating barrel for the pond in the field, painted it with black tar, and made an oar to propel it. He made up a circus all on his own, made the clowns' clothes, wrote the words and played all the parts. He was always rushing, always thinking, and his wise parents let him have his head. The youngest boy was David, and there was no nicer, kinder lad in Cornwall. He was polite and friendly, and never stopped smiling. He had none of Gerald's brute strength, or Dennis' drive but he was loved by everybody and a pleasure to be with. Finally, there was the only girl, Peggy. Not only was she the youngest, but also she was as cheerful as David and as combatative as the rest of them, and nobody seemed to notice that she was only a girl. Their mother had been a nurse, and was a capable, caring person, taking her share of farm work as well as bringing up a thriving family. They all adored her.

Mr Prophet, the farmer, was a remarkable man. He was tall, and had huge sloping shoulders, with forearms like hams and fingers like sausages. His round, red face was marred by a harelip, but it never bothered him. He said very little, preferred his wife to do the thinking, and worked like a horse, from dawn to dusk, every day of the week. He milked twenty-one cows by hand, and strode behind his big carthorse with leather straps around his shoulders to guide the plough, never stopping, or saying anything, apart from uttering strange commands to the horse when the beast was required to turn or to quicken.

I was with the family one day when he ploughed up an entire field of potatoes single-handed. Peggy and the boys, poorly assisted by me, were there to collect the potatoes, put them into sacks, and drag the sacks to the edge of the field so that Mr Prophet could collect them later in his "wain", a high-sided cart, drawn by his horse which did all the heavy work. I do believe Mr Prophet could have pulled the wain himself if it became necessary. We children soon lost interest and began to throw potatoes at each other. Mr Prophet untangled himself from his harness, came across and gave David and Gerald a meaty clout. Dennis and Peggy had already disappeared, and, as a visitor, I escaped with a fierce glare. Then he got back behind the plough, wound the reins around himself, chirruped at the horse, and away he went again.

The horse and the wain, and the pony and jingle, were all the help Mr Prophet had on his farm; there wasn't even a tractor available. Yet he worked tirelessly, like an indestructible robot. His strength was colossal; he threw full milk churns around as though they were cans of baked beans. He once told me how he had nearly got to the Great War in France. He was called up in Redruth, marched as far as Salisbury Plain, only to hear that the war was over and they could all go back home. I had my doubts about marching all the way from Redruth to Salisbury, but such was my awe of Mr Prophet's physical power and stamina, that I knew he could do it easily if so ordered.

It seemed to me that everything on that farm was busy and bubbling. The family loved one another, stood up for each other at school, were as lively as children could be, and yet were never rude or ill mannered. They showed affection easily, cuddled their mother, pulled their father's leg, and had their own pulled in return. I always waited to be invited to visit them, and never failed to be overjoyed when I went. But my spirits soon drooped when it was time to return to that grim and cheerless house, standing among the stark ruins of a dying industry.

One day, the Prophets surrounded me as I entered the school gates, and seemed very excited about something. They said their mother would like it if I could call in for a cup of tea on the way home. It was obvious that something unusual was in the air, and I guessed that it involved me. After school, Peggy and David escorted me back to the farm. They wore huge, toothy grins, but in spite of my pleading, they would say nothing about why I was being invited home by them in such a joyous fashion.

Mrs Prophet made me sit down and gave me a huge slice of currant cake. Then she told the others to leave us alone together. She began to talk to me, and I knew that she must have been an excellent nurse because she was so patient and understanding, and made me do much of the talking.

"How do you like being evacuated?" she asked. I said that I missed my mother and my father, and my family, and all my friends at home, but sometimes I was fairly happy.

She thought for a moment, as though she wanted to ask a delicate question but hadn't made up her mind how to frame it.

"You seem to enjoy yourself here, with the children," she said. I replied that coming and playing with the others on the farm had now become the happiest part of my days in Cornwall.

"Are you very happy where you are, down the road?" she asked. I suppose I must have tried to remain a little loyal to Mrs Wally, who was insensitive rather than uncaring, and saw to it that I had enough to eat and that my clothes were tidy when I went to school. I certainly said nothing in praise of Wally and his father. I must also have said that it was not a very happy household anyway, and nobody seemed to laugh or enjoy life. In fact, I was growing more and more sad as the days went by, but I had resigned myself to the situation, as I had learnt to do through those uncertain and dangerous days and nights in the Bristol bombings.

Then she came to the point, suddenly and exquisitely, and I shall never forget my joy when she said, "Do you think you would be happier if you lived here, with us, as part of our family?" I couldn't believe it. I pretended not to understand, and she repeated it. Would I be happier with the Prophet family? It was delight so far removed from possibility that it had not for a moment crossed my mind.

My face said everything. She said, "We'll go and pick up your belongings, then."

"Tonight?" I asked incredulously. David and Peggy tumbled in at that point. They had obviously heard everything, and their mother didn't seem to mind.

"It's all arranged," she smiled, and the three of us galloped down the hill together to the row of houses. Wally's mother was expecting us. My bag was ready, together with one or two items which I had made at school. She said her goodbyes, with no more passion than she had shown on the day I arrived. Wally lurked half hidden by the front door, and said nothing. Back we skipped to Little-beside-farm, and I led the way exultantly in through the front gate of the farmhouse. The sun was still shining brightly, and there were chickens on the lawn, and hens scratching away in the under-growth. The front door opened and Mrs Prophet gave me a huge smile and a hug of welcome. Gerald grinned awkwardly; Dennis stopped what he was doing for the briefest moment and a smile spread over his face. Mr Prophet stood at the porch, his legs wide in his wellingtons, his fists on his hips and his old cap dangling from one hand. "Yoo'm welcome, boy," he said, and that was as genuine a speech as that strong man was capable of making. I put out my hand to him, and he buried it in his own huge paw. He put on his cap, and wheeled away, smiling and shaking his head, back to his labours.

As for me, I turned and saw the evening clouds drifting over a soft sky, and the green fields and hedges stretching over the hills, and the ancient grey granite walls threading in every direction; and I knew there was not a happier boy in the whole of Cornwall.

16

The Prophets' farmhouse must once have accommodated a live-in servant, because there was a discreet second staircase at the side of the entrance hall. But the front of the upstairs part of the house had been turned into one long dormitory. The boys had their three beds in a row, and to them was added a single bed for me. There was a fifth place, at the other end, which had a curtain around it, and obviously that was for Peggy.

They threw my gear onto my bed, and we tore back downstairs and out onto the garden. It was towards sunset, but still very light, and they showed me where the chickens scratched about on the lawn, and how they laid their eggs in secret places in the hedges and the undergrowth. My job would be to hunt out the eggs and put them carefully into a basket for Mrs. Prophet. This was one of her own private enterprises. She also kept bantams, and there was a prize angora rabbit in a hutch. Its wool was supposed to be very expensive. I could help feed the chickens, clean out the rabbit hutch, and make myself responsible for egg collection. The kitchen garden occupied one side of the house, and was also Mrs. Prophet's domain, although she expected everyone present to do the labouring for her. I would do anything to please that lady, but my assistance was reckoned to be a little dangerous as well as costly, since I launched into the work with plenty of action but little idea of what was a plant and what was a weed.

At the rear of the farmhouse were three tired apple trees. They were gnarled and stained green, and had long ago ceased bearing worthwhile fruit. Dennis, in his ingenuity, had turned them into an assault course, with a wooden platform in the branches of the biggest tree. He had driven six-inch nails into the trunks, and ropes were suspended to assist the climber. Dennis could twinkle around it like a monkey in the Monkey Temple at the Zoo in Bristol. When I tried, I got stuck halfway up a tree, and was too frightened to go on or go back. Dennis was at my side in an instant. He didn't shout; he remained calm, and explained in a normal voice what I should be doing. I refused to give up, and completed the course at last under his encouragement, though with aching arm muscles and scratches all over. Once again I marvelled at the incredible leadership powers of Dennis, who seemed instinctively to know how to react in any situation.

There were twenty-one cows to be moved into the farmyard and milked at least once a day. We all lent a hand at collecting the cows, although it was easy enough, really. The beasts knew instinctively when the time for milking and feeding had arrived, and they all knew where to go.

Peggy teased me and said I would be too scared to try milking one for myself. She was more right than she knew. The last time I had tried to milk one of God's creatures was the disastrous episode with a billy goat engineered by Wally. I inspected the cows. They all had huge, rolling udders, and four teats each, correctly located. Mr. Prophet had washed them clean and was sitting under the haunches of one. He was tugging rhythmically, and spurts of milk were hitting the bottom the bucket he held between his knees. He had rather a high-pitched voice for such a powerful man. He looked up and shouted, but never paused in his stroke. "Peggy! Give'n a bucket and stool, and show'n what to do."

Peggy was delighted, and I was given a three-legged stool to sit on, and shown how to nudge my shoulder up under the cow's rear leg, and get to work. I looked at the creature, and she swung her huge head away from the trough of hay and regarded me carefully through soft brown eyes. I took that as a warning, but I grasped two of her teats and gave a tentative pull. Immediately she knew that she was literally in the hands of a dilettante, and jerked smartly on her halter. Mr. Prophet was rising from his stool with a bucket full of warm milk, ready to be poured into the churn. "Leave'n bide," he said sharply, and I was grateful to hand over to the grinning Peggy, who set to work at once with the skill of her father.

I only remember speaking to Wally once in all the time I remained in Cornwall. It was in the schoolyard, and in his usual sarcastic way, he said that he supposed that I was now living off clotted cream and plenty of meat. Quick to spring to the defence of the Prophets, I began to say how much I enjoyed the cream that Mrs. Prophet could churn out in the dairy. Immediately, Dennis, with his quicksilver mind, was into the conversation, and explained that I was talking about the odd tin of condensed milk which we had been using. Nobody was convinced, but Wally remained silent. It would have been a poor farmer's wife indeed, who couldn't supply some cream to her brood, no matter what the rationing laws said.

Life with the Prophets was not only highly enjoyable; it was also intensely amusing to a city lad who had been taught (especially by Mr. Taylor at Victoria Park School) to observe and question everything.

I noticed, for example, that although Mr. Prophet's day was one long round of hard work, it was far from unplanned. He was governed by the seasons, and by the weather on the day itself, but he was still well organised, and always had a job in hand if he was unable to start the one he had planned. He knew how to make every minute work to the extent of hiring himself out for the day to another small farmer. He didn't always expect payment; sometimes he required a return favour from the other man, to be called in when warranted. This happened when he wanted to remove a tree from the top field. There was a large sycamore that was taking up too much room. One morning early, his neighbour arrived, and we all set to work. Mr. Prophet marked out where he wanted the tree to fall, and soon they were busy lopping off limbs, and then branches, and dragging them away to make room for the hard work. They used a six-foot long two-handed saw, and a 14lb axe, and a sledge-hammer with a steel wedge, and sawed and cut and hammered that tree until at last it crashed to the ground exactly where Mr. Prophet had planned. Then Mr. Prophet sent Gerald to put the tackle on the carthorse, and he and David dragged the log out of the way until it was needed. Meanwhile the rest of the men (and boys) dug under the stump, exposed the roots, and cut and hacked at them, until the horse could be attached and it was finally dragged out of the ground to leave a wide, clean-smelling hole. This was filled in and turfed over, and Mr. Prophet had won about a quarter of an acre of extra land to work with. And, right on cue, Peggy and her mother arrived with scalding pots of tea and sandwiches and slices of home-made cake. We sat where we could, and fed, and grinned contentedly at each other, as if we had single-handedly dismantled the Empire State Building.

I rapidly learned that, although they loved animals, they were strictly part of the capital assets of the farm. They still called cows

91

names like Daisy and Buttercup, but they were there as milk-producing units. If one got ill and couldn't be saved, it was replaced without a tear or a moment's hesitation. Apart from the hens, the bantams, and the rabbit, they had a great carthorse, which pulled and pushed and strained all day until let out to graze. They also had a pony, which was kept to pull the "jingle", the farm's only form of transport. There was not a car nor a tractor nor anything mechanical in the whole enterprise. The only animal to be treated as a pet was a strange looking dog, which they called "Demo". It was ages before I discovered that this stood for "Democrat", which was part of its long pedigree title. It was short, with stumpy legs, a long body, a bulbous wet nose, and ridiculous ears, which were like velvet pads and hung almost to the floor. When it was not covered in mud, because it was so near the ground, its colour was a beautiful mixture of cream and tan, and it had big, sorrowful eyes. Demo was everybody's pet, and there was no doubt that if she departed, tears would flow like water.

I also gained a feeling for how ancient place names were derived. The field with the pond was called "Pondfield". There was "Top end", "Bottom End", and the meadow in front of the cowsheds was called "Barn field". I don't know how the strange name "Little-beside-farm" came about, but I'm sure Mr. Blewitt would have known. He was the headmaster of St. Day Village School, although I did not see much of him because he was often ill. He told us why Cornish place-names often sounded biblical. This was partly due to the fact that in ancient times, small communities called themselves after saints (like St. Day) in order to be under holy protection. He also said that the Phoenician traders came from the east and bartered their own wares, like oils and cloth and perfume, for Cornish tin and perhaps dairy products. These traders came from biblical lands, and left their names behind. Mr. Blewitt told us that the most common name in Cornwall at that time was Williams, because many of the miners, who came over from South Wales to work the wheals, or mines, were called Williams.

No one took holidays. Mrs. Prophet had some relatives "up north", which didn't mean Yorkshire or Scotland, but "North Cornwall", which was "up" Bude or Padstow way. Mr. Prophet sometimes took us to a sale, if he wanted some second-hand equipment and a chance to chat with fellow farmers about the market and the weather and how badly the war was hitting them. There was the occasional foray into Redruth, and this was regarded as a holiday in itself. We got up early and queued at the bus stop at the top of the lane. The road wound through the beautiful green countryside, which I had already explored extensively. I knew as well as the others where the sweet little wild strawberries could be found, and how to catch a flock of grazing rabbits unawares, and send them hurtling down their holes, their white scuts jerking behind them. I knew where there were secret brooks, and green-coated ponds, and thick bracken where you could lie motionless in the tall green ferns, and hear strange, unidentifiable movement all about. I knew where insects hummed and buzzed, and how to turn over and gaze up at the lazy-pacing clouds as they strode, gigantic and silent, across the clear blue sky above. Always, on these occasions, my mind turned to a snatch of one of Miss St. Hill's poems:

Where the grey trout lie a-sleeping,
Up the hill and over the lea;
That's the place for Billy and me.

But I didn't need the presence of any "Billy". I could manufacture and enjoy my own dreams. I felt the same when I wandered up the wooden stairs to the old barn where Mr. Prophet kept his mixtures for adding to the cows' food, with the aid of a galvanised metal scoop. I could watch a rat scuttle across the gaping floorboards, or see the rain trickle in through the leaking roof, and land in powdery bursts upon the dusty floor beneath. In all this I found exhilaration I had never known before, but which I was reluctant to mention, even to the Prophets.

Redruth was a town on a hill. At school, I could sing "Trelawney" (Here's twenty-thousand Cornishmen shall know the reason why!) as lustily as any Cornish lad. I could also sing "Goin' up Camborne 'ill, coming down!" but I had a suspicion that this did not, as was suggested, refer to Richard Trevithick's steam engine, which was on display in Redruth, but something more risqué. But we were there to go to the cinema, and specifically to see Will Hay and his "schoolboys". It was hilarious. I found myself sitting on something sharp, and discovered it to be a stoutly made catapult, no doubt the pride and joy of a previous customer. That was a bonus. When we met at the bus stop to go home, you could almost see Dennis' mind turning somersaults, and he was the first to climb on board. When we got home, he rushed straight to his cupboard and produced paper and pencil from which he began writing a script for us all to perform, in his own version of Will Hay and his dreadful school and pupils.

I had spent some time using his drawing and writing materials. Like all small boys in Bristol, I had seen sketches of the outline of various friendly and Nazi aeroplanes, and we were encouraged to recognise them. I don't quite know how that helped the war effort, but I became quite a star with my ability to sit at the kitchen table, close to an oil lamp, and produce Spitfires, and Heinkels, and Blenheims, to order. But never did I hear an air raid warning, although there was some talk once of some bombing "down Falmouth way". When I told Mr. Wally about spending twelve hours on end in an air shelter, he practically told me I was lying. Even my new friends didn't take it too seriously, so I didn't press the point. But I was well aware that the real war was not in the remotest way apparent around St. Day.

High summer came, and was marked by "Feast Day" in the playing field alongside the road to Truro. This was the Feast of St. Day, and the entire village turned out in their best clothes to watch the children play organised games, and talk to neighbours, and generally enjoy a rare chance to meet each other. Mr. Prophet didn't come. He loved his farm, and never left it unless it was absolutely necessary. In any case, there was always so much to do if you worked a farm single-handed. Even Gerald was given time off only grudgingly.

The climax of the day was when the vicar said a few words and we all queued up to receive a sixpence and a saffron cake. This was a Cornish traditional food that I never grew to like; but I took mine, and ate it, just to show that I was as Cornish as they were. But of course I realised that my few months in the Duchy would never qualify me to be a local.

I loved my life in Cornwall and I am sure that had Mrs Prophet not been so insistent, I would have not been so scrupulous about writing letters to my mother every week. Of course I still loved her, but she was miles away, and I was in the middle of a new life and enjoying every minute of it. I thought always of my father, and sometimes of my brother George at Perranporth. I had heard nothing about him since the day they took him away. I could barely recall the faces of my two young brothers, at home in Bristol. All I knew was that the bombing had practically ceased since the day George and I had been evacuated.

Summer came to an end, and autumn came in with rain and storms and gales from the sea, which was only a dozen miles away, east or west. The Lizard Peninsula, and Lands End itself, the last outcrop of England, was a bare forty miles away, and the rain swept up in brooms across the velvet green of the fields, and the iron-and-chalk coloured barrows. There was talk of early snow, which sent Dennis speeding to the barn to build a sledge in anticipation. The boy at the next farm had brought in his new pony for us to look at. We all enthused. I was shoved up into the saddle and told to ride down the lane. I was terrified; it was like sitting on top of a wardrobe. The ground was miles below me. The leather creaked and rubbed my thighs, and the stirrups were too long for me to reach. The last thing I wanted was to ride that pony, and the animal knew it, and I was thankful to be helped back to earth again by all the young experts.

Every farm had a working pony; although I never saw the Prophets saddle their animal. They went everywhere in pony-and-jingle, a small, high-wheeled cart with rounded end and a dangling cast-iron step for boarding at the back. The driver sat in front, usually sideways on, and used the long whip and a set of peculiar noises to encourage the pony as it clattered along those country lanes. It usually took a passenger and a couple of milk churns to the raised concrete plinth, which was the milk collecting point on the Truro road, used by all the farmers.

I was standing in the lane, watching Mr. Prophet loading up the jingle, when Mrs. Prophet called to me. I followed her into the house, and immediately knew that I was about to hear something serious because she led me into the sitting room, which was only used on special occasions, such as talking to "Maister", one of the big farmers, or welcoming visitors from Up North.

"I've had a letter from your mother," she said, "And the bombing in Bristol has almost stopped. We both think that it is time for you to go back to your family."

I was thunderstruck. I had never supposed that the life I was leading could ever come to an end, and yet I was sensible enough to realise that I had not been sent to Cornwall for a holiday. Sooner or later I must go home.

"Don't you want me here any more?" I asked. But that was not fair, and I knew it. This kind lady had four growing children, a husband who never stopped working, and she had taken me in without a question when her children told them about this unhappy evacuee living just down the hill. She left me alone in the sitting room, and the others were told in loud whispers to keep away for a while. I soon had it clear in my mind, and when I went back into the living room everyone was looking at me anxiously. Even Demo's eyes seemed to have got bigger, and heavy with sympathy.

We didn't waste much time after that; obviously my mother and Mrs. Prophet were well ahead with arrangements already. I left the next day. I stood at the gate, my belongings already packed, and waited for Mr. Prophet to bring the jingle to take me to Redruth. I looked down over the green fields, with the low clouds trailing drizzle like cobwebs, the breeze gentle, and the air still mild for November. The rain had varnished the burrows, and smoke rose vertically from the chimneystacks in the cottages by the old mine workings. David and Peggy were there to see me off; Peggy wreathed in smiles and wiping tears from her eyes at the same time. And good, loyal, David was standing there looking miserably at me, unable to find any suitable words to fit the occasion. Mr. Prophet brought the jingle to the gate with a clatter, and stopped to allow me to climb in using the footplate. Everyone shouted goodbye – and then, as the pony gripped the lane with its hooves and began to pull away, David tried to give me something. He ran behind the jingle, and tried to climb in. The sudden extra weight was too much for the pony, and its eyes began to roll like big black marbles, and its ears stood up like carrots. "Geddoff!" yelled Mr. Prophet, but David persisted, and the pony was taking one step forward and pawing at empty air at the same time. "Get -OFFF!" screamed Mr. Prophet, and he half-turned from the front seat, where he was desperately trying to control the pony. He swung around and dealt David a frightful back-hander across the face, which sent the boy rolling into the ditch at the side if the lane. He rose quickly, and held up a hand in which he held a letter for me. We were disappearing rapidly, and I never read it. We waved to each other silently, all the way to the main road, and the white envelope was still waving forlornly as we passed out of his view.

We rattled on into Redruth, Mr. Prophet and I not speaking because he was not a talkative man. He helped me down from the jingle, took my bags, and paid the ticket office man the money for a single journey to Temple Meads station, Bristol. Then, his task completed, he turned and looked down on me, his feet apart and his huge fists on his hips.

"Goodbye, boy," he said. "You'm a good 'un. We'm gonna miss· 'ee." I gazed at him, looking up into his brick-red face, his hare lip, and the keen appraising look, which went through you like a knife even when he said nothing.

"You'd betterway 'ave some money in case you gets 'ungry," he said. He reached into his working trousers and pulled out two half-crowns, which he handed over quickly as though not wanting to be noticed. "P'raps you'll come and see us again, later on."

And that was enough of being sentimental. He was away on the jingle, without looking back, and I wandered resignedly into the waiting room for a train to take me back from whence I came, seven months previously.

17

My mother was overjoyed, and it took me all of a minute to feel thoroughly at home, although it took me longer than a week to get used to it. She showed me a copy of the letter she had written to Mrs. Prophet, thanking her for looking after me. Her last sentence stuck with me always: "I pray that, one day, you will have, not "Little" beside-farm, but "Much" beside-farm." That was a very pretty way of putting things, and I knew Mrs. Prophet would be delighted.

My younger brothers, David and Philip, were also probably pleased to see me, but at their age it was difficult to be certain. Meanwhile I had a spot of unfinished business to attend to. Across the road lived the Little family, and the youngest daughter was a very pretty girl called Maureen. She had asked my mother my address in Cornwall, and had very kindly written to me to cheer me up. Rudely, I had not replied. I was very much afraid of girls, and had this feeling that if I wrote back, Bisto Smith and his gang would find out and I would be jeered at for "going out with a girl." I saw her in the street, and she took the fight straight to me.

"You're ignorant!" she said; and in the way she meant it, I certainly was. I tried to explain my feelings, but my reasons didn't sound convincing even to me. To her they were totally unacceptable. She sniffed, tossed her black hair back, and walked away. Apart from crying when all the kids made me kiss a girl in a doorway at Catherine Mead Street when I was five, this was my first involvement with the opposite sex. I felt I had lost this battle conclusively.

I waited for the baker to come with his horse and cart. Seven months in the country had made me a son of the soil, and handling livestock was no problem to me. I went to stroke the horse's nose. It reared up, terrified the baker who hit me with his basket, and deposited a huge, steaming pile of rose dressing noisily on the road. My mother shouted at me, the baker yelled at her and me, and I was left recalling that I was the one who had tried to milk a Billy-goat, couldn't milk a cow, and had been terrified when lifted onto the back of a very docile pony. How quickly one's aspirations are shattered.

Other attractions had grown up in Lynton Road while I was away. St. Hugh's Church, "missionary" sister-church of St. John's in Bedminster had started a Wolf Cub pack. I first heard of this through Bisto Smith, who spoke with savage satisfaction of the games they played. My mother said I could join as long as I stuck at it. She had no time for people who carelessly chopped and changed. I was greeted by Akela and Bagheera, two nice ladies who attempted to run the pack between them. They told us that they were named after characters in Kipling's *Jungle Book*. For the most part, having these two ladies in charge was about as effective as putting two maiden aunts into a cage of lions, in an attempt to instil discipline. Every session began with a game of "British Bulldog". This was not because Akela, the cub mistress, was particularly fond of the game. She just resigned herself to the certainty that the evening would never start unless the boys could play "British Bulldog" first. What a magnificent game it was, too. We were divided into two teams, and sent to opposite ends of the hall. On the signal "British Bulldog", you launched yourself at the opposition and attempted to break through their ranks to the other end of the hall. Then you turned around and tried it again, until all of one team had been captured. Those were the rules – plain and simple. What went on to achieve these ends was incredibly violent. As each successive attack was launched, the opponents howled like Zulus at Rorke's Drift, and rocketed at the opposition. No matter that the floor was wooden and inclined to splinter; forget that the wooden chairs that lined the hall made excellent weapons. Even the Light Brigade could not have improved on these bloodcurdling, headlong dashes at the foe. If Waterloo was won on the playing fields of Eton, "British Bulldog" must at least have influenced the battles of the Somme. The havoc continued long after Akela began to plead for her charges to desist. "That's quite enough for this evening boys," she would plead despairingly, and quite without optimism. But enough for our lads was when we were fully satisfied that old scores had been paid off, some blood had flowed, and at least one or two of the wounded had fled home in tears. Once let slip, the dogs of war were hard to recapture. Only when we were really satiated would we consent to stand in line, grinning happily at each other, and wondering how we were going to explain away torn shirts to mothers with very few clothes coupons, and hardly any money, to spare for financing our contests.

The next most favourite game was "chucking kneelers". The church was built on very sparse lines, and little money had been spent beyond what was absolutely essential. There was hardly any cupboard space, and any equipment was stored at the back of the hall behind two velour curtains. Piled behind the curtains were the hassocks, "kneelers" as we called them. They were bulky oblongs of tightly packed velvet, made especially for small boys to sling at each other. This activity was strictly forbidden, and regularly practised. The piles of hassocks, neatly stacked ready for the next service, were waiting there all ready to be used. When the fit took us we would disappear behind the curtains and emerge with an arm full of kneelers, with which we bombarded friend and foe alike until a weeping Akela finally restored order.

The worst sin we could commit was to ring the church bell. At the other end of the hall was a wooden roller-screen, which protected the altar when the hall was in use. This was flanked by two doors. One led to the vestry, and if you knew where the incense was stored, you could have a wonderful time, trying to push it into the shaker, light it, and whirl it around your head to create a highly satisfactory smell and volumes of smoke. The other door opened into a small room in which a bell-rope dangled through a hole in the ceiling. At crucial points in the church service, a trained ringer would give the bell a tug, and its single note would echo solemnly up Lynton Road and across the Novers. Both doors were kept locked, but a simple door-lock was scarcely likely to deter a well-educated boy from Lynton Road. Sooner or later somebody would get in, and give the rope some hearty heaves, sending erratic signals in all directions. Inevitably the culprit was caught red-handed, and he would be sent home immediately. But the punishment never matched the crime, and the sheer bliss of making music with that bell, especially when it was so strictly forbidden, more than compensated for having Cub Night suddenly terminated by a distraught Akela.

So popular (or notorious) did Wolf Cub nights become, that Father Stephen, the priest-in-charge, began to take a lively interest in what was happening among the deprived young innocents of his flock at St. Hugh's, Lynton Road. He was a sincere, dedicated cleric, but his years among the dreaming spires of Oxford had done little to prepare him for labour amongst the self-regulating families of Bedminster, Bristol 3. He was middling tall and slightly tubby, as though he had eaten too much at school. His hair was waved, and he wore horn-rimmed spectacles, which shielded his constantly sour expression, as though there was always a faintly unpleasant smell just under his nose. His dog collar was shining white, his long cassock hung down to his well-polished shoes, and a narrow black leather belt bulged rather too much at the middle. In uniform he was a caricature of the perfect scoutmaster, even to the forked thumb-stick he carried to Cub Nights, much to the infinite joy of the locals. They applauded his progress along Lynton Road, where he looked as out of place as a tap-dancer on a tombstone. He looked even chubbier and well nourished in uniform. He was slightly too perfectly dressed, with his well-shaped scout's hat, his pressed neckerchief, his polished waggle, and his long socks, which were folded down at just the right length, with a correct glimpse of a green tab visible. He did little more than open and close the meetings, with prayers delivered in a highly parsonical voice, which we all found most fascinating.

He announced to us one night that "Next Tuesday is the day of a very special saint, and there will be Mass said at 9 in the morning, if we can be there."

That was when I had one of my brainwaves. I persuaded several of the lads that, if we went to this service at 9 in the morning, we could be away from school for a couple hours, and nobody would dare touch us because we had been doing something holy. So half a dozen of us marched into St. Hugh's Church on Tuesday morning, to the great astonishment of Father Stephen, who could rarely get as many of us to attend on a Sunday. The service over, we dawdled off to school, but as we frittered away the time we began to realise what lay ahead of us. Mr. Taylor was not one to be deluded easily, and when we saw him waiting for us at the school gate, our courage began to fail us; when he politely invited us into his study, it vanished altogether.

"Been to Church have you?" he enquired, looking deeply interested. But you could tell he didn't really expect an answer.

"Very praiseworthy, I must say. Off you go to Church, don't tell anyone where you are, and I'm left with a half-empty school and my staff out looking for you." Mr. Taylor was always a supreme canesman, but today he was in England form. We got three of the best on each palm, and I got one extra for leading the plot. He

101

wasn't even out of breath when the final blow had whistled down on the soft pink flesh of the last errant hand.

"Perhaps you will talk it over with me first, next time you feel this overwhelming desire to go to Church on a school day," he said, and we all filed out and re-joined our classes. I was sure he gave me an especially hard look. He had his own way of encouraging promising boys, but favouritism was an unknown word in his vocabulary.

18

At last my father came home on fourteen days' leave. We reckoned we could hear the click of his army boots as he turned the corner from Dawlish Road and marched smartly up Lynton Road towards us. My mother had left the front door ajar, and this time we really could hear him, striding up the path. Suddenly, he was among us, with a broad grin and his brown eyes shining with delight. He wore a greatcoat and a forage cap, which he quickly snatched from his head and flung into a chair. He looked fit and vital; his brasses and buttons were gleaming, his gaiters were blancoed to perfection, his toecaps shone like black glass, and you could cut string on the crease in his trousers. Over his shoulder was a canvas kit bag, with his steel helmet wedged in the top. And over the other shoulder was slung his rifle. A real rifle, big and heavy, the stock stained brown, and the lock and the barrel a dull, oily black. I was absolutely fascinated, and tried to lift it. My father took it from me with a laugh. "Thank you, son," he said. "That goes upstairs until it's time to go back."

He took off his greatcoat; there was a lanyard around one shoulder, and it disappeared into one of the pockets of his battle-dress. His wore his regimental tabs and epaulettes, and a patterned design on his sleeve. I was so proud of him I could have burst, and I knew at once that all I ever wanted to be was a soldier; a general, for preference, after a bit of training. He reached into an inside pocket and pulled out some money and some ration cards. "Credits," he said, "for my leave." We asked the inevitable question.

"How long are you home for, Dad?" His smile disappeared, and his face became thoughtful.

"Two weeks, son. This is embarkation leave."

"What's embarkation leave?" My mother already knew, and supplied the answer.

"Your father is being sent abroad, so they've given him two weeks leave to say goodbye. He doesn't know where he's going, so don't ask him. We've got him all to ourselves for a fortnight, so let's enjoy it."

The first thing he did next day was to catch the train to Cornwall to rescue my brother George from where he still languished, in a hostel at Perranporth. Apparently it was quite an experience. With no opening pleasantries, my father said that he had come to take his son back to Bristol with him and the train left in half an hour. Kindly get his things together. The staff said they couldn't possibly do that, what with all the paperwork, and the short notice, and everything. My father went purple. "I am home on embarkation leave, and you talk to me about paperwork. You are wasting my time. Kindly fetch him at once." At least George reported that was roughly what my father said, as far he could remember. I have no doubt there were many gaps to be filled in the exchanges. I never heard my father swear in all my life, but I imagine he was close to it that day. They caught the train, and George's recollection got a little hazy then. He said the compartment was full of servicemen, and when they heard about what had happened to him over the last few months, kit bags were emptied and chocolate and sweets were produced from nowhere. My brother was magnificently sick by the time they reached Plymouth, and slept for the rest of the journey. My father must have told the story dozens of times before his leave ended, and he grew more pleased with himself every time he told it.

My mother sent a note to Mr. Taylor, and I was allowed out of school to be with my father for a few days. We walked for miles together, and I was immensely proud of this smart man in uniform as I tried in vain to match him stride for stride. I suppose it was because he was on embarkation leave, and didn't know when he would be back, or even if he would be back; but he seemed very anxious to visit the places he knew so well. We walked down to Catherine Mead Street, which was now notched with gaps which were once houses. We passed Mr. Boyd-Joll's, the dentist, who had pulled all my father's teeth out in one go on a Saturday morning.

We walked down North Street towards Ashton, turned on the road to Clifton Suspension Bridge, and reached the Clanage, the home of Bedminster cricket club. We looked over the long wall at the empty field where once our doctor in Catherine Mead Street had been a star player. The lower of the two pitches, the one nearer Clifton Suspension Bridge, had been requisitioned by the military, and was now the site of a balloon barrage unit. Where the "A" team used to play, there was now a Nissen hut, a cookhouse and an ablutions block, for service personnel. Floating under the restraint of a thick cable was the barrage balloon itself. It was huge and silvery, filled with gas, and shaped like a whale with the drooping ears of an African elephant. When the air-raid signal sounded, this balloon, and many like it around Bristol, would be allowed to soar into the sky with the hope that enemy aircraft would fall foul of its cable.

The top pitch was intact but overgrown. It was hard to picture the strong Bedminster side of just before the war, playing cricket in this jungle. I thought of names like Tom Adderson, the Home brothers, Ron Gillett and Wilf Pont, Edgar Gillette, Aubrey Simons and his father Jim, Tommy Allen and others, with Reg Whittle behind the stumps. You had to arrive very early on a Saturday to get a seat, or even a place to lean your elbows and look over the wall. Now it was deserted, except for some aircraftsmen going about their duties. The wooden pavilion in the top corner was not even required, and stood, forlorn and empty, waiting to be of service again.

We turned and went back towards Ashton Court, the great home of the Smythe family. Lady Smythe (as we called her) used to own the Clanage, and was President of Bedminster C.C. Every year, she summoned the Chairman and the Secretary to the Court, where the butler admitted them. They were given tea in the library, after which she wrote out a cheque for half a guinea as her annual contribution to the funds.

We strolled for a minute or two alongside the famous "seven mile wall", a ten-foot high masonry wall which enclosed the estate. Bristol City footballers traditionally ran around this wall – past the Clanage, up Rownham Hill, left along Beggarbush Lane, left again and back to the City Ground – as part of their training for a new season. At the end of the lane turning into the drive which led to the Court itself, there was a sentry box. In it was a soldier, leaning against one side and reading a paper. His rifle was resting against the wall behind him. He looked up, folded his paper, raised a languid arm, and said, "Hi, there!" I thought a touch of the "Present arms" and "Halt! Who goes there!" would have been more appropriate, and looked at my father for guidance. "He's American," he said quietly, as if that explained everything. He began to talk with him. Quite soon they were discussing English currency. My father asked him if he understood it, and when the American looked at him suspiciously, as though he was about to be robbed, my father laughed and said that English money could be difficult for a foreigner to get used to. Pretty soon they had all the coins of the realm out and were passing them to each other, my father explaining their comparative values. Then the American produced bank notes, including a five-pound note, of which I am sure my father had only seen one or two in his whole life. The American was huge; they all seemed to be much taller and rounder and thicker than English soldiers. He had a splendid olive-green uniform, a strangely shaped tin helmet with the chin straps dangling loose, and a glorious array of ribbons on his pocket. On his sleeve were two lots of chevrons, smaller than those of a British N.C.O., and worn upside-down. He didn't wear gaiters; instead he had a pair of laced leather boots, which reached halfway up his shins.

He and my father became more relaxed, and the American, in the voice of a cowboy, said he was sorry he had no chewing gum to give me, but offered my father a Camel cigarette instead. My father declined and said that, with the greatest respect, he would rather smoke nothing than smoke a Camel. I guessed they must have been pretty bad, because my father could not exist without his daily ten Star or Woodbines. When we said we had to go, the American thanked my father warmly for his help, waved his arm lazily, and sank back, as if exhausted, against the wall of his sentry box, his hands in his pockets.

I urgently drew my father's attention to something I thought he must have missed. "He's *black*," I whispered when we were out of hearing distance. My father said, "All his unit are black. The Americans keep all their black troops together, and his lot are billeted in Ashton Court."

The inevitable "Why?" rose to my lips. Mr. Taylor had taught me well, but hadn't fully explained that close questioning sometimes brought dire consequences.

"It's the way they do it in the American Army," he said. "It just wouldn't do to have a black soldier in a position senior to a white one, and be able to give him orders." I could feel the "Why?" rising again, but suppressed it. I could see that my father had not worked this out to his own satisfaction, but clearly felt that there was something wrong about the situation; so I let it pass.

We walked on in silence until we got to Ashton Gate, the home of Bristol City Football Club. This was my team, as opposed to Bristol

Rovers, whom my father supported, since he was born on that side of Bristol.

"City are playing there on Saturday, and Ronnie Dix will be turning out. We'll go, if you like." Ronnie Dix was one of Bristol's famous players. I had never even been to the City Ground, but I knew all about Ronnie Dix and Clarrie Bourton, and Cliff Morgan, Ernie Brinton and Alfie Rowles, and other local heroes. In fact, Fred Pincott lived next door to us for a time in Catherine Mead Street. It was wartime, and, for the duration, teams were picked according to who was home on leave. Sometimes, quite well known stars, stationed locally, were prepared to turn out for City or Rovers. I once saw an Irish International goalkeeper called Hugh Kelly playing at Ashton Gate. He wore a bright orange jersey and a flat cap, and must have been in his prime several decades earlier, because he was as big as a house, with his belly flopping over his knicks, and his face as red as a beetroot.

The day was wet and the surface of the entrance was liquid ash. I went to use the urinal, and was almost sick. The floor was streaming, the drains were blocked, and an endless queue of men paddled to the stalls, and left as hurriedly as possible, buttoning their flies on the trot as they went out, all the time puffing furiously at their Woodbines to disguise the stench.

When the game was over, we forced our way out of the narrow space between the half-open iron gates, and joined the stream of spectators marching homewards. "I didn't see much of Ronnie Dix," I said, expertly, to my father. "You couldn't have been watching very closely," he replied, "he scored a hat-trick." I comforted myself that I couldn't really see much of the game anyway. We were leaning on a crush barrier under the Wil-Sam-Mor stand, and every time any action came our way the crowd surged forward like a huge wave. I was too busy staying alive to pay too much attention to details like Ronnie Dix's hat-trick.

As much as I enjoyed my father's leave, each day finished with the realisation that there was one day less to go. Soon time was up, and we watched gloomily as he packed the last of his kit into the cylindrical kit bag. He kissed us all, hugged my mother, and slung his rifle over his shoulder. I could smell the shaving soap and feel the rough serge of his greatcoat as he embraced me, and thought how smart and alert he was, even at such a sad time.

"I'll write to you as soon as I can, and tell you where they sent me," he said to my mother, and marched down the path, along Lynton Road and down Dawlish Road until he was out of sight. He never looked back, but we strained to hear the sound of his steel-tipped boots receding into the distance. That was the last we saw of my father for over a year.

My mother said father had given her the money for us all to go to the pictures that afternoon. I didn't believe my father had that much money to spare, but I knew that my mother wanted to take our minds off suddenly being without a father for a long time, and possibly for ever. With my parents, optimism was one thing; realism was quite another. We went to the "Town Hall" and saw a Tarzan film. My brothers enjoyed it, but my mother and I were glad to sit in the dark and compose our thoughts. When we got home, the house seemed terribly lonely, and we went to bed quietly, and with a newly empty chair in the living room.

19

With my brother George back at home, my father gone indefinitely, and two small brothers to help look after, life had to be organised, otherwise it would become chaotic. To supplement what money my father sent home from the army, my mother went out charring two or three time a week. In her absence I was responsible. This meant, in the endless grind of her life, that she couldn't do everything, and if anything went wrong in her absence, it was my fault. My first task was to light the fire every morning. This meant shovelling out the dead ashes from the night before, wrapping them in newspaper, disposing of them in the ashbin, and starting a new fire for the day with paper and kindling wood already prepared. This happened while my mother made breakfast and looked after the babies. George and I saw ourselves off to school, and when I returned in the afternoon, I had to ensure that the place was in some sort of order for my mother's return. Often the back door was locked, but entry was easy if you pushed a newspaper under the door, and wriggled a twig in the lock until the key could be pushed through. It then fell onto the waiting newspaper, which was pulled carefully back out and the key retrieved. Many houses used to leave the front door key hanging inside the front door, tied with a piece of string to the knocker on the letter-box. When you wanted the key, you just hauled it out, used it, and re-threaded it back through the letterbox. I don't recall any crime-waves sweeping Lynton Road as a result. The lads were far from innocent, but stealing from neighbours was not in their repertoire of villainy.

Once a month, Mr. Andrews, who lived two doors away, would cut our hair. George and I would knock at his kitchen door, and see if it was convenient. "Give us ten minutes," was his invariable reply; which meant he wanted a quick fag first. When we came back ten minutes later, we took it in turns to sit on a chair in his kitchen, and have a grubby cloth tied around the neck. We would plead with him not to cut too much off, but it never made the slightest difference to the result. His routine was unalterable. He never spoke; he executed a quick dash across the top with comb and scissors, a rapid flourish down the sides with the clippers, and when he had seen to us both he said, "tanner!" So we gave him our sixpence and he returned without a word to the living room and sat there in silence.

When we got home my mother examined the result very carefully, and sniffed in derision. "Call himself a barber?" she snorted. "I could do better myself, and save the sixpence. I'll tell Mr. Andrews so, next time I see him." But she never did. His scullery might not have been a hairdressing salon, but it was quick and cheap, and was all my mother had the time or the money for.

I was beginning to observe things which I had not really noticed before. Why did small groups of men sit in the field by the Novers, up against the hedge, and play card games for money on a Sunday morning? What did Alf Brook do when he and Molly O'Grady went up the Novers, towards the stone butt, in the dark, and come back arguing about money? And why did Mr. Thomas always sleep under the hedge outside his front door, when he came home drunk from the Engineers' Arms every Saturday night?

I also had my first experience of a serious fight between two women. It was not uncommon to see two men fighting, particularly when the pubs closed. It was Double-British Summer Time, which meant that the clocks had been put back by two hours. It didn't get dark until after 11 p.m., so you could see all these things.

As I passed the flats at the bottom of Lynton Road, towards Parson Street, I noticed a crowd had gathered, and they were cheering two women at the top of the stairway. The flats were on two floors, and the concrete stairway and iron banister to the upper dwelling was on the outside of the building. One of the women was stocky and very excitable. She had ginger hair, and she swore blue murder. Much energy was spent in threatening her opponent with what she would do with her once she had caught her. She seemed to be getting the better of the contest, because she was doing all the work, and tugging the other in all directions, legs and arms flailing like windmills.

The other woman was calm, and almost dignified. Her face wore an angelic smile, marred only by a bright scratch down one cheek. Gradually, though, the tide of the battle turned, and the quiet lady slowly took charge. She began to batter the ginger lady, but her sweet smile never left her face for an instant, and gradually you became aware that this was a mask of total wickedness.

110

Ginger turned on the steps, and slipped, and the crowd roared as the other woman leapt on her in an instant. She grabbed her hair, she punched her, and kicked her, and tried to bite her, until the crowd turned uneasy, and then angry, and finally dragged her off. I ran straight home and told my mother about this dreadful experience, but, to my surprise, she didn't seem at all put out. I knew that it was just not acceptable for two women to fight in front of others like animals, and I was astonished that my mother made no comment. But by now I was beginning to know what a clever mother I had. If she had gone into the matter in detail, she could have underscored it for ever in my impressionable mind. Instead, she chose to brush over it, and treat it lightly, so that I would not be troubled for long. Besides, I reflected, coming from the dreadful slums in which she and my father had been raised, she would scarcely have been shocked. She would certainly have witnessed sights more frightening than two women fighting in the street.

My father was not the only soldier in the street. Maureen Little's eldest brother had been called up, and very smart he was too. So were the fathers of several other children, but the soldier that the King would miss least of all in his army was Alfie Brook, Alf Brook's father. Alfie was a skinny, greasy little man, who never walked when he could slink. The whole family were incredibly dirty, and their front garden had lost all its privet hedges and was a flat waste of earth, bicycle frames, tin cans, and all types of assorted rubbish. Mrs. Brook was huge and unwashed. Her body was as thick as a mattress, and her arms were heavy and coarsely red. Her face was fat and pasty, and her eyes were black, malevolent slits in a wicked countenance. Her eldest son was Alf, who was doing his best to sink to his father's standards, and succeeding ignobly. Her youngest son and her infant daughter were mentally sub-normal, and were thrashed so often that they were terrified of everything and everybody, and were too frightened even to speak. Her eldest daughter was also mentally limited, but all the neighbours were fond of her, and did what they could to help her, without inviting the vengeance of her mother. Finally there was the eldest-but-one daughter, who was growing up to be the image of her mother, but with far more intelligence, which made her many times more dangerous.

The army had seen fit to pluck Alfie out of this squalid brood, with the purpose of making a soldier of this dreadful man.

Somehow or other he passed the medical, and after missing a few initial appointments at his Training Centre because of flu virus, or "didn't receive the letter", he presented himself for treatment. This began a long series of episodes which, did the War Office but know it, raised the morale of the good people of Lynton Road to an enormous extent.

We began to look forward to the cameos; the plot never varied and we were rarely disappointed. We waited until Alfie came home on leave, politely enquired how long he would be home for, and sat back to see what would happen. The time for returning to his Unit would come, and, unerringly, go. Meanwhile Alfie spent all his money and whatever he could borrow, down at the Engineers' Arms. If he got drunk, he would give his wife a beating. When he became sober, she would whack him. At last the climax would arrive. A jeep would draw up outside the front gate, and two immaculately uniformed N.C.O.s from the Military Police would march up the steps and bang hard on the front door. Eventually, Alfie would poke his head out, all bleary-eyed, and ask what the trouble was. When he was told that General Montgomery was missing him badly, and would like Alfie to return to his Unit and give him some advice, he would feign innocence. "Din't you get my letter?" he would demand in astonishment. "I must 'uv phone the Guard Room at least free times! I bin bad, like."

It never worked from the beginning, and the M.P.s eventually used to join in the charade. They called him "Alfie" and pretended to be sympathetic, promising to put in a word with General Montgomery on his behalf. The conclusion was always the same. Alfie was sent inside to pack his kit, and would come out minutes later with his battledress unbuttoned, no tie, greatcoat over his arm, and trailing socks and dirty underwear down the front steps to the waiting jeep, while the neighbours cheered him all the way. After the first visit the M.P.s wouldn't even go into the house. It was not only because Mrs. Brook stood on the doorstep and bellowed at them ceaselessly, like a cow in agony; but because it would have been preferable to wallow in a pigsty than to enter Alfie's place of residence. I thought it was very funny indeed, but my father, when he heard about it, was far from amused. To him, military discipline was sacred, and certainly not a matter to be taken lightly.

10. Hitler couldn't stop play: street cricket in Temple Street, Bedminster after an air raid in 1941. Bob Flower, the author's lifelong friend, is fielding at short square leg, on the right.

11. Down the steps to the crypt under St Pauls' Church, Coronation Road, Bedminster: shelter to hundreds of Bedminster folk during the blitz.

12. Apprehensive children being evacuated from the city. This picture was banned by the censor as not being cheerful in adversity.

13, 14 & 15 Little beside-farm, St Day near Redruth, where the young John Budd spent a happy few months. The lawn where he saw the chickens is off to the right. Opposite, at the top, industrial remains and, bottom, the road from St Day to Truro. The witch's house on the left, track to Little beside-farm on the right.

16. Lynton Road, Bedminster.

17. The Malago from Parson Street, Bedminster.

18. Up the steps to Merrywood Grammar School, now gone.

20

I was now thoroughly enjoying being a Wolf Cub. Brother John had been drafted in by Father Stephen to assist the two well-meaning but nervous ladies who were meant to be in control. They were as timid as sheep, but the woman in charge paradoxically insisted on using her *Jungle Book* name of Akela, the Wolf, with Bagheera as her faithful assistant. They were ostensibly in control, but the discipline they could provide was hopeless in Lynton Road. Brother John rapidly gained the respect of all of us because he was strong, could out-run us, and played British Bulldog with us in a way which brooked no bullying unless you were prepared to receive an elbow from him in return. He also inspired loyalty in a way which was impossible for the ladies to imitate. I became a second-sixer, with one yellow band on my arm; then a sixer, with two bands and the charge of a "six"; and, finally, a senior sixer. This made me the senior Cub, a position of which I was immensely proud.

But, far more importantly, even at the age of ten, my "promotion" began to unfold for me the first germs of the problems of being in charge. In Lynton Road, boys couldn't easily be bullied. They could be encouraged, cajoled, pleaded with, or ignored. Each boy was different, and I soon discovered that three yellow bands on my sleeve meant nothing in themselves. Imperceptibly, without even realising it, I was experiencing the skills of leadership. To be liked was fine, and, to a degree, could be purchased. But to be respected was infinitely more precious, and beyond price. My headmaster, Mr. Taylor, had no favourites. Neither did it appear obvious that he wanted to be liked by his pupils; but he was liked by most of them, and enormously respected as well. You could buy a temporary sort of liking from your companions in all manner of ways. But respect you could never buy. In Lynton Road, kindness was often mistaken for weakness, so you might as well be straightforward from the outset. I suspected that would be true wherever I found myself.

Brother John said to me one day that it was almost time for me to leave the Wolf Cubs and become a Boy Scout. He said that Father

Stephen would like to talk to me about it, and had arranged for me to visit him at St. John's vicarage. This was almost as far as the London Inn, and I hoped the journey would be worthwhile. When I arrived at the old grey house, I knocked at the big, brown door, and it was opened by an ancient lady with a spotless pinafore and suspicious eyes. She looked sourly at me, glanced at my shoes to see that they bore no unwelcome luggage, which would defile her scrubbed floors, and showed me into Father Stephen's study. All was dark brown, and sombre. Two of the walls were lined with bookcases, as tall and as long as those in Marksbury Road Library. The books were mainly bound in dark leather, and there were many different versions of the "Holy Bible". There were crucifixes hanging on the walls, and pictures of Jesus, from His birth, His boyhood in the Temple, to His Ascension. And there were Sunday school texts, greatly enlarged and embroidered, and suspended from all manner of places. Massive plum-coloured curtains, which were themselves half drawn, protected the windows and the lights were heavily shaded, adding to the gloom of the atmosphere. I began to wonder why everything to do with the worship of God had to look so desperately miserable all the time.

Father Stephen rose from the chair in front of a brown writing desk, and greeted me. He seemed much more confident, here on his own territory and away from the wild horde of boys in Lynton Road. The flash of his glasses was a reflection of the sombre yellow lighting. As usual, his hair was immaculate and his dog collar gleamed white. He was dressed in his long, belted cassock, but I noticed, as he stood up, that he wore his full-length Cub socks.

"Would you like a glass of milk? he asked politely.

"No thank you Sir," I replied. Small boys, unless they are forced to drink it at school, do not generally like glasses of milk. A large glass of orange squash or red Tizer would have been very welcome, but I wouldn't expect Father Stephen to know that. He sat me down in the corner of a large, brown, leather settee, and I was promptly swallowed up. My feet didn't reach the ground, a cushion toppled over onto my head, and I felt as though I might gradually sink out of sight altogether into the belly of this huge piece of furniture.

"John," he said, thus putting me on my guard immediately. Grown-ups seldom used the Christian names of children. When they did, it usually meant they wanted something. "Thank you for

114

coming. You've been an excellent Wolf Cub, and we want you to become a Boy Scout. The Troop at St. Hugh's is run by two very dedicated young men, and I'm sure they would welcome you."

I nodded. When dealing with grown-ups, the best way was to say nothing, but to listen carefully until they had finished talking. If you committed yourself too soon, they would usually spring the unpleasant bits on you after you had agreed to everything else, and it was too late to negotiate.

"You will be taught how to do your Duty to God and the King, and to help other people, like old ladies, and to be useful, and to obey the Scout Law." He then went over the Scout Law in detail, and I groaned to myself. I knew that I could never promise to be as dutiful, kind, helpful, polite and courteous as General Sir Robert Baden-Powell, the Chief Scout, had prescribed. I listened to his litany of the unachievable with a rapidly sinking heart, and began to wriggle to the edge of the sofa, ready to get up and leave when I could do so without offending him. Then he said, "I have obtained for you a copy of *Scouting for Boys*, which is Baden-Powell's handbook of Scouting. You may keep it if you wish."

On the way home, I began to read that book, and by the time I got to Lynton Road, I was captivated. So much of it appealed to the private life which I preferred to lead. I loved to walk alone over the Novers and out along the Malago valley, and sit silently where I couldn't be seen, and observe what was happening about me. Here was a book, which told me how to do it properly, written by a man who had done it himself, during the wars in South Africa. It told you that you tell a man's character by looking at the heels of his shoes. If he hadn't cleaned them, he was not to be trusted. Neither were people who wore silly quiffs in their hair, or whose eyes were too close together. I could tell which way a cyclist had ridden by looking at the tracks to see how they converged; he was always riding the way the long, thin loop pointed. I already knew, and had it confirmed for me, that the best way to remain invisible was to stand perfectly still against a matching background; it was amazing how few people were able to use their eyes. I played "Kim's Game" all on my own, putting a dozen or two different articles on a table, looking at them for a minute, then looking away and seeing how many I could memorise. I tried to become observant, and to learn what I could about other people by studying them closely. This in turn taught me not to be too observant, because large, healthy men often resented having a small boy suddenly appear and commence staring at them.

There was also much I didn't understand in the book. There was half a chapter on "Beastliness", and several pages on "Continence", and the more I guessed at the meaning of these headings, the more sinister they seemed to become. So I dropped this branch of my studies, and stuck to matters which struck a chord of fellow feeling in me. Thus, when Ern and Ivor received me at the next meeting of the Scout Troop, I was well indoctrinated already.

Ivor was a tall, blond, studious young man, who wore his Scout Leader's uniform meticulously, and whose main role seemed to consist of confining Ern's boundless enthusiasm to the limits of what was feasible. Ern was dynamic. Nothing was impossible in his eyes, and with the help of Ivor, he succeeded in raising the ambitions and expectations of that tough bunch of lads in Lynton Road to an astonishing level, given their backgrounds. After all, they expected very little from life in the first place, and were very rarely disappointed. Ern was full of energy. He was crazy about speedway racing, and loved football, though he didn't do much of either himself. My mother, polite, but worldly and tough, insisted on vetting Ern before I was enrolled into the Scouts. Her main condition before she allowed me to undertake anything was that I would stick at it. If I joined, I stayed, until she saw a reason why I should leave. And she was very careful to subject whoever was in charge, to a very close scrutiny. There was no problem with Ern; his enthusiasm and his decency were transparent, and she liked and trusted him immediately. He was powerfully built, not very tall, and had a slight stammer. He lived with his mother and sister in Weymouth Road, and adored them both.

Obtaining a uniform was a problem; the hat, neckerchief, waggle, belt, shirt and trousers, were more than my mother could afford in one go; so Ern bought the lot for me, and my mother gave me as much as she could spare, on top of the weekly "subs". Every week Ern would refuse to take the money, and every week my mother would insist that he did, and the charade continued until the last payment had been made.

Ern was not very strong on "Scout Law" and promises to King and Country. But he knew all about enthusing the boys. He had little problem with the football team. Ray Boucher, Kenny, Jackie King and few others, were natural footballers. But there more than a leavening of Bisto Smith's assassins in the team. Th. opposing Scouts had led normal lives, and had never encountered the likes of Bisto's mob outside of a Zoo; the fear they inspired in the opposition was awesome. They were sufficient to terrify a platoon of the Grenadier Guards. The footballers in our team had little trouble in clearing up, once Bisto had completed his demoralisation process.

My particular pal was a cheeky, skinny boy called Wilkins. He was not exactly the type that Merrywood Grammar School was seeking to build its future on, but on the other hand, gaining a place at Merrywood did not figure anywhere in his own list of ambitions. He could see the funny side of anything, and to be near him for the evening was a tonic. He regularly escaped the blame for his atrocities, because nobody could believe that a boy with such an angelic smile could possibly be the culprit. We both sang in the church choir, and with his white cassock, his scrubbed face, and his beautiful voice, he could charm the very Saints themselves. He regularly infuriated Ern, who often chased him all around the church hall, down Lynton Road, and sometimes halfway up the Novers, seeking revenge after yet another outrage.

We vied with each other in the gaining of badges, and Wilkins was incensed when I got my Firelighters' Badge before him. We had to light a fire with one match, out in the country, using the thin bark of the silver birch tree instead of paper, together with whatever kindling wood we could find. I had it on the authority of the Chief Scout himself that a scout should always "Be Prepared". I knew that silver birch trees were not commonly found in Lynton Road, or even beside the Malago at Bishopsworth, so I had "prepared" myself by tearing out half the back page of the *Bristol Evening Post*, and hiding it ready for the test. With the aid of the newspaper, one match was more than sufficient, and in no time I had a roaring fire, which Ern insisted on showing to all the aspiring Firelighters, as an example of what could be done. When Wilkins howled his protests that I had used paper, Ern told him to shut up and stop being so jealous. Wilkins gained his badge the following week by using my own underhand but effective tactics himself, only in his case, he was not cheating, but improvising.

117

Our next target was the "Athletes' Badge", and we needed to qualify in the high jump. The ever-enthusiastic Ern immediately volunteered to open up the church hall especially one morning, and show us, personally, how to do the high jump. Unfortunately, St. Hugh's Missionary Church for the poor and deserving of Lynton Road had no money to spare for sophisticated high jump apparatus, so Ern brought a length of his mother's clothes line. He tied one end to the top seat in a stack of wooden chairs, and told Wilkins to hold the other. He glared ferociously at Wilkins. "Don't forget, Wilkins", he threatened, "If I catch my foot in that rope, LET GO AT ONCE! Otherwise I'll go flying and bring that stack of chairs over on top of me."

I distinctly remember thinking at the time that to tell Wilkins what disasters might ensue if he held the rope too tight, was taking just a teeny bit of a risk. However, the first two or three jumps were completed successfully, and Ern, thoroughly enjoying himself, shouted "Higher!" Whereupon Wilkins gave the rope an extra pull to raise it a few more inches. Again Ern was successful, and brim full of confidence. Triumphantly, he called out, "O.K., Wilkins; right up, as high as you can!"

We watched this final, prodigious effort, with interest. Ern went as far back as he could, right back to the vestry door, while Wilkins held the rope in a slack hand. Ern sucked in several mighty breaths, and fixed his gaze on the rope, concentrating on it with fiercely knit eyebrows. Then he took a final, huge, lung-full of air, and suddenly powered himself away from the wall behind him, using the sole of his foot to give himself extra velocity. He ran like a terrified stag, and his knees and elbows pumped in all directions. His teeth were bared, and his eyeballs spun around in their sockets as he strained every muscle and sinew to get at that rope.

It was obvious that he wasn't going to make it. This was the point at which Wilkins, had he obeyed orders, should have released the rope to allow Ern free passage for his long flight through the air. But Wilkins didn't let go. He held on tightly, and Ern screamed in terror as his ankle was held and wouldn't let his body pass through. He performed a magnificent somersault, and crashed onto the wooden floor, with the stack of chairs hurtling down on top of him, seeking to bury him beneath their sharply projecting legs.

"Wilkins! *Wilkins!*" shrieked the shattered Ern, as he examined his body for signs of broken bones or gushing blood. "WILKINS!"

he howled again. "Come 'ere and I'll *kill* you!" But Wilkins had vanished out of the side door and was, at that moment, hanging, helpless with laughter, on the gate outside. I was convulsed, but dare not let Ern see, lest he throttle me where I stood. Ern was sure he had suffered at least three severe fractures, and staggered shakily to a chair, where he sat for a while, quivering more in rage than in pain. He kept saying "That flippin' Wilkins!" over and over again. Steam rose from his damp forehead, and sweat trickled down to the end of his nose and dropped off like tiny crystal marbles. I did offer to fetch him a glass of water, but the look he gave me convinced me that he was already certain that I was in league with Wilkins over this act of attempted murder. I hadn't been, but I thought it best not to discuss it in detail at that juncture. Instead I trotted prudently home to read *Scouting for Boys*. It was some time before the matter of the "Athletes' Badges" was raised again.

21

No properly brought up child from Bedminster will forget the annual Sunday School Outing to Weston-super-Mare. Our Sunday school was in the Chessels (Chessel Street) and the Superintendent was a most remarkable Bristolian. Alderman Charles Gill was a one-time Lord Mayor of Bristol, and leader of the mineworkers in Bristol. He was short, stout and balding, with a dark suit and a gold chain draped over the front of a bulging waistcoat. When he spoke, he murdered the English language; but his air of authority was unquestionable. It was he who arranged the annual outing to Weston.

There was little chance of a real holiday for many people in Bedminster, and the Sunday school day out was looked forward to for weeks beforehand, as much by the mothers as the pupils. The evening before, everyone had to go to the church hall and collect their tickets, a sixpence, and a voucher to go to the tea party in the afternoon at Weston. The applicants were carefully scrutinised to ensure that they really were Sunday school members, and the precious little green cardboard train tickets were handed over. Above all, we were told to behave or we would be sent home. How exactly that was to be achieved, nobody mentioned. Then Mr. Gill said a prayer for our safety. I sometimes thought that, to be absolutely on the safe side, he ought to add a few words to secure the protection of the unsuspecting townsfolk of Weston-super-Mare, who were about to have Bisto Smith and his pals descend upon them.

Next morning we were up and about early. My mother packed sufficient equipment and provisions to meet any eventuality, and we set of for Parson Street Station. We ran up and down the wooden steps from the street to the platform, and generally occupied ourselves dangerously until the specially booked train arrived with much puffing and hissing of steam. It had left from Bedminster Station, one stop back, and was already half full of people from other Sunday schools in Bedminster. The doors were wrenched open, and we poured in, to the amusement of those already on board, who had taken the best seats. Slowly the train gathered pace, and we chugged towards Weston, shouting out the names of the stations as we shot past them. Flax Bourton, Nailsea and Backwell, Puxton and Worle, and, at last, Weston, where the carriages disgorged and we flooded out onto the pavement in Locking Road. Small boys were there with homemade carts and dandies, ready to take holidaymakers' baggage to their boarding houses for a few coppers. They knew every bed-and-breakfast, from "Dunroamin"' to "Mon Repose", as well as a London cabbie knew the "knowledge". But they had no interest in us, nor we in them, and we surged up the main street until we could see the entrance to the Grand Pier ahead of us. The pace of the crocodile quickened, and we chased across the road.

The next part of the ritual now was to see whether the tide was in or out, and to do some careful calculations concerning when it would be high tide, and thus be enabled to swim. The first hour was one of endless excitement. The air was clean and fresh and you could smell the sea and the sand. Flatholm and Steepholm, the two ancient islands, stood out in the channel, the final giant steps of the Mendips as they struggled free of the grey rocks of Brean Down, and strode out towards Wales on the far shore.

There was so much to do that we scarcely knew where to begin. Mr. Trapnell's donkeys, small and uncomplaining, were lined up, ready and waiting for their endless hundred-yard saunters. Just over the sea wall, on the beach, dozens of stalls stood invitingly. You could buy shellfish, including winkles with pins provided. There were cockles in china dishes on the narrow ledges of the stall, with unlimited salt and vinegar and pepper, there for the shaking. There were buckets and spades, wooden or metal; and paper flags and windmills, and cardboard hats with elastic chinstraps and cheeky slogans, and bats and balls and rubber sea shoes, and hoops and sticks, and Diablo, and hooters to blow. There were kiosks, which sold tea by the pot (deposit on the tray, returnable). Everything that was vital to a real day out was there, on display and open for anyone with pennies to spend.

There was the drinking fountain where you could queue for ten minutes to depress the lever and slurp up a few mouthfuls of water, taking great care not to touch the metal with your mouth for fear of catching some dreadful disease. And, lording it over the other attractions was the entrance to the Grand Pier. It was guarded by even more stalls, and "Guess your weight" merchants, who took a penny off you and gave you a farthing ring as a prize if they were wrong; and "talking" weighing machines, which spoke your weight, or shot out a printed card which told you your weight *and* your fortune, all for a penny.

It cost another penny to breach the turnstiles and have the glories of the Pier opened for you. It was a wooden structure, supported by hundreds of rusting iron stilts that marched miles out into the sea. There were seats on both sides, and a glass wind-shelter ran its whole length down the middle. At the far end, standing like a huge be-flagged box in the distance, was the Mecca of our journey, the Fun Fair. Can there ever have been so many delights under the same roof to transfix small boys with their splendour and diversity? There were slot machines, which, for a penny, would spring into life and show you the death of Charles Peace the murderer, or the execution of the condemned convict in the electric chair at a place called Sing-Sing. Graves would open to disinter glowing yellow corpses; or you could witness the downfall of a gentleman to death through drinking. If you could get up onto your tiptoes, you could jam your forehead against an eyepiece, turn a handle, and see "What the Butler Saw", which usually wasn't much, because the sepia photographs which flicked around in sequence inside the ancient machinery were practically invisible.

There was a large, evil-smelling, oily pool, around which motor-boats chugged in serene circles at their own pace. Or there was the satisfying fury of the "Dodg'ems", vicious little electric two-seater vehicles, driven by power, which ran from the car through a steel pole to a connection above into the electrified wire-mesh ceiling. You controlled your speed by a throttle pedal, and your direction by the steering wheel. It was padded all round because collision was the name of the game. There was a twin objective; you either rammed somebody, or you avoided being rammed by somebody else. Nobody ever went on the Dodg'ems just for the ride.

There were distorting mirrors, and the Crazy-house, and the Ghost Ride; and, swooping up and down, high above everything else, was the loop-the loop, which hoisted you up to the roof so that for a brief moment you could look down on the sideshows. Then it hurled you down, and around frightening bends, so that your stomach was left far behind, and you were secretly grateful when the ride was over. And the noise was deafening; hurdy-gurdies, and huge loudspeakers relaying the Andrews Sisters and the Inkspots in millions of decibels, and the shouting of barkers, and the screams from all those subjected to the tortures of the careering and clattering mechanical contraptions, and the smack of air-gun pellets on metal back-plates – all combined to produce a deafening and unending cacophony of sound.

Back on the beach, the mothers had assembled deck chairs into circles, like wagons on the prairie, each group consisting of friends and neighbours. We joined them there, and braced ourselves against the stream of cautionary remarks, as mothers strove to outshine each other in displays of wisdom and prudence.

"Don't get sunburnt. Keep out of the wind or you'll get heat stroke; I don't want you up all night crying like you did last year. Keep your hat on, or you'll get sunstroke and be sick. Don't fling the sand about so."

And then the tide would come in; swift, long, shallow wrinkles of muddy brown water, each billow no more than six inches high, but as thrilling to us as the ocean rollers of Bondi Beach would have been. The sea advanced in irregular carpets, melting the sandcastles and filling the holes we had so carefully dug. The bold among us ran out to meet it, and danced in with it. The apprehensive ones stood in their demure swimming costumes with shoulder straps and long legs, and shivered, knees bent, toes turned inwards, arms across the chest, thumb in mouth, looking abject and miserable. And then, as the tide turned and began to recede as rapidly as it arrived, mothers would order their offspring to "get in and wash the mud off before it's too late."

At lunchtime, one of the great traditions of Weston-super-Mare was scrupulously observed. Mothers would dip into purses, produce some coins, and say, "Go over to Coffin's and get the fish-and-chips!" There were never, anywhere in the whole wide world, fish-and-chips to match those produced at Coffin's on Sunday-school outing days. Brown, crisp, and steaming hot, so that you had to blow on them in case they burnt your tongue.

"Plenty of vinegar, mind; no salt on Albert's. Double chips for missus. D'you want cod or haddock, Gran? Come straight back, and don't lose the change." When we had queued with the dozens of others sent by their mothers to fetch Coffin's ambrosia, we raced back to the camp to find that somebody had already fetched a tray of tea, and somebody else had produced a bottle of red Tizer, to be passed, hand to hand, for a carefully measured swallow. It bubbled down the throat like cold boiling water, and left a lipstick stain on the mouth. The wind drove the sand like whips. It got into your eyes, into your hair, and, no matter how careful you were, it got into your fish-and-chips, so that you could feel a crunch as you took a bite.

"Stop throwing the chip paper around. Collect it up and shove it in the bin, you untidy little monkey." Instructions, instructions; always there were instructions, but a child's mind is built to sieve instructions carefully before they reach the brain, so that they can be acted upon or ignored, as he sees fit.

Suddenly it was time to pack up and wander to the church hall for tea. Organisers demanded the vouchers, most of which were produced. The food was laid out on long trestle tables, and kind ladies came around with huge enamelled brown teapots. The handles were huge, and the curved spouts had "V"s cut into the ends. The food was mostly currant buns and cake and sandwiches, but we were more keen on quantity than quality, and it was an act of duty on the part of each of us to eat as much as possible before the plates were emptied. Then it was time for the organisers to make a speech, say some prayers, and urge us back towards the station in plenty of time for the train. The enthusiasm and excitement of the morning dwindled in the tired acceptance of a day coming to an end as the crocodile made its untidy way back to Locking Road. Bisto Smith and gang had to be carefully rounded up and corralled, to prevent them saying reverent thank you and farewells to bewildered local youngsters, with the aid of fists and boots. The train was already at the platform, growling and steaming with impatience, the guard looking at his watch and shrugging helplessly at the driver. There was little skylarking on the return journey. Tired trippers were happy to relax and reflect upon the day. Never mind that my brother George had crimson shoulders which he couldn't bear to be touched; or that Margaret Chilcott's nose was bright red; or that Raymond Williams had lost his cap; or that Les Phillips wanted to be sick and the toilets were full and a queue was waiting. Going home was now the main preoccupation, and when the train slowed down and released us with a final admonitory huff and puff, we were only too anxious to climb the wooden stairway into Parson Street. We meandered home as the sun set in a reddening sky. Our backs itched, our eyes were sore from the sand, and the road seemed twice as long. This morning our steps were light; now our feet were heavy as lead as we trudged back to Lynton Road, which we had left, twelve impossibly short hours ago.

22

Maurice Marks and I were the stars at Victoria Park Junior School; at least, as far as Mr. Taylor would allow "stars". If you got a little above yourself, he had an uncanny habit of kicking the ladder away, until you acknowledged that you were part of the school, and that it didn't exist merely to indulge you personally. We confidently expected to be chosen for Merrywood Grammar School. We knew we would also take exams for Queen Elizabeth's Hospital, but we had no intention of succeeding, because it was the custom of that ancient school for some of the boys to wear black tunics and long yellow socks. Life would be hazardous enough as it was, to be pupils at Merrywood. Bisto Smith and his pals would make it quite unbearable if I came home dressed in a Q.E.H. uniform resembling girls' clothes. We would also sit exams for Bristol Grammar School, but we were Bedminster boys, and if we were to go to a superior school, tradition demanded it had to be Merrywood Grammar School for Boys, perched high on the top of the Novers.

In the final examinations before we left Victoria Park, I came top and Maurice Marks came a very close second. Either one of us could have been first, but the surprising element was that, although my English was better than my Arithmetic, and his talents lay the other way around, I had beaten him in Arithmetic and come second to him in English. We both took the examination for Merrywood with little fear of the outcome.

To the astonishment of everybody, certainly to me, I didn't pass first time. Maurice Marks romped through, but I had to go before a panel of teachers for an interview to see if I was worth a place. Mr. Taylor called me in, and was very kind. He said that some people were not brilliant at passing exams and unfortunately for me, in his opinion I was one of them. However, I was to present myself personally to a panel of teachers at Southville School. They would question me, and read his own evaluation of me at the same time. If I came through this successfully, I would have passed the examination and would go to Merrywood with Maurice Marks and, no doubt, some others from Victoria Park.

He told me what time to get there. "Go to bed early the night before," he advised. "Add up the figures on your bus ticket; do anything to be sharp when you go to the interview." I was grateful to him for his care, but I knew there would be no adding up of bus ticket numbers. As usual, the family budget would preclude me from such luxuries as bus rides. However, I could do a great deal of "sharpening up" as I walked along Marksbury Road, across the tip, up Sheene Road, over North Street, and to Stackpool Road and eventually to Southville School.

The panel were a kindly bunch, and certainly had no plans to catch me out with trick questions. We just talked to each other; and then a lady asked me what books I was reading at the moment. My mind suddenly froze. I had read enough books to fill Marksbury Road library twice over, and I couldn't think of one title or one author, not even Richmal Crompton. In desperation I had a sudden flashback to Miss Greengrass' shelf of "new" books, and I recalled that one of them was written by Nigel Balchin. I couldn't even remember the title, but I blurted out "Nigel Balchin". To my enormous relief, the interview suddenly finished at that precise point, and I was out in the street again, remembering books by the dozen and kicking myself for being an idiot.

I told Mr. Taylor about this a day or two later. He said, "Don't worry; some boys have passed the interview." *Some* boys! And he looked at me so oddly that I reddened and was glad to get away. At the end of the week my mother received a letter to say I would become a pupil at Merrywood in the coming September. I couldn't wait to tell Mr. Taylor.

"Congratulations, Budd," he said. "I told you *some* boys had passed; do you see now what I was trying to tell you, so that your mother wouldn't worry?" I pretended I understood him from the very beginning, and I thanked him. But I didn't really know he was trying to tip me off. Perhaps it had something to do with my difficulty in passing exams first time. But I was well aware, when I trotted out of the front gate of Victoria Park School and into St. John's Lane for the last time, that I was leaving behind me, not only an extraordinary teacher, but an example which I would do well to follow closely, and a human being whom I would never forget.

23

The mystery of where my father had been sent to fight the war was soon solved. His letter arrived, covered in deletions in red ink made by the army censor. "Careless Talk Costs Lives," we were being told repeatedly. And yet, in spite of the crossings-out, my father still managed to tell us that he and his unit had been sent to Lerwick, in the Shetland Islands, which was as far north in Britain as you could get. He described the long rail journey, followed by a terrible sea crossing, which made them all seasick, and how they were billeted in some Nissen huts, on the top of the cliffs. He said the huts were exactly the same as those we had seen on Bedminster's cricket ground at the Clanage, and it made it much easier for me to visualise. He said that the storms could be fierce, and the gales were sometimes as strong as 100 miles an hour, with waves as high as Wills' factory. At other times, the sky was beautifully clear, the air was calm, and he liked to sit on the cliffs and look out towards the mainland, and imagine that the war was over and he was at home with us. He said that his unit had actually shot down a German aircraft, and the C.O. had come to congratulate them personally. I couldn't help wondering how that item of news escaped the pen of the censor; perhaps it was a fiendish ploy on behalf of counter-intelligence or misinformation, to let the Germans think that my father was up north, shooting down their aircraft by the dozen. He enclosed a photograph of himself and another soldier, playing draughts on his bed. My father was a fine draughts player, and none of us could ever beat him. When my mother saw the photograph, she said she would go out and make a cup of tea. George said there was no need; she must have forgotten that we had only just had one. I shut him up at once. I knew my mother wanted to be alone for a moment.

Air raid warnings were now irregular, and never seemed to amount to much these days. Food and sweets and clothes and everything else were strictly rationed. There were some strange new foods appearing; Spam, tasteless tinned meat, was the one I hated most. Unknown fish became available, and powdered egg, which I thought was not at all bad when made into a sort of omelette. We also had plenty of orange juice, which came in medicine bottles, and was supposed to provide vitamins. This was just about acceptable; but the liquid made from hips, was awful. My mother also made us take a dessert spoonful of Cod Liver Oil and Malt every day. It was like runny toffee, and tasted of nothing at all. The problem was, it took a long time to disappear down the throat, and while you were waiting you were in real danger of bringing it all back up again. But my mother said that it did us good, and we couldn't argue anyway, so we just queued up and literally took our medicine.

We were fortunate indeed that my mother was such an excellent cook. She could make a meal, and produce another meal the next day, which was entirely different from the first, but made from the leftovers of the same ingredients. No food ever seemed to go into her larder, but always enough came out to feed and satisfy us all.

Christmas came around, and that was when I missed my father most deeply. But my mother refused to let us become morose. She began to make cloth dolls to sell. She shaped them, and I stuffed them with flock, and painted eyes and a nose on each papier-maché face. Then my mother dressed them beautifully, right down to miniature knickers. We stayed up late, working to order, but selling them at a ridiculously low price, in my opinion. We went up the Novers, and brought back sprigs of evergreen. We cut up paper, made paste out of flour, and produced paper-chains, which we hung in great loops all around the living room. The previous occupants of the house had obviously had a small Christmas tree, which they replanted, in the garden. We dug this up, put it in a bucket with some earth to keep it solid, and out-did each other in devising Christmas decorations for it. Because we had never had very much, we didn't expect very much, and what we did have we had supplied all on our own, which made it that much more enjoyable.

We did our share of carol singing to make the odd penny, went to Sunday school Christmas parties, and looked out for Mr. Payne's car. Mr. Payne was a friend of my father, and he had the baker's shop where Cannon Street turns into North Street. Without fail during the war, he would drive up Lynton Road a day or so before Christmas, and slip a brown envelope into the letterbox. On it was written "Happy Christmas to the Budd family." In it was a ten-shilling note, and this made all the difference between a happy Christmas, and a luxurious one. Mr. Payne never waited to be thanked, but we always wrote to him in gratitude; I don't think he really understood what an immense difference ten shillings made to our Christmas enjoyment.

Traditionally, on Boxing Day, we went to British Road in Bedminster and had tea with my mother's sister, Auntie Jessie, Uncle Fred, and my three cousins, and Gran, my grandmother, who lived with Aunty Jessie. Also among those present would be my Aunty Harriet and Uncle George, who was Uncle Fred's brother. He was a lay preacher, and had a truly hearty smile, and a loud, Father Christmas-type laugh. My cousins were terrified of them, and if they dared think of missing Sunday school, they were threatened with the wrath of Auntie Harriet.

We would all troop down Marksbury Road, up Shepton Walk, and across Bartlett's Bridge to arrive in time for tea. Certainly Auntie Jessie did her best for us all, and there was no shortage of Christmassy food and drink. Then we would start the games. There was "spinning the plate", where you spun a plate in the middle of the room and left it as long as possible before you called the name of the person who was to catch it before it actually stopped spinning and flattened onto the carpet. George and I were far more agile and determined than our cousins. Where we would leap, they would lunge, and then cry, "cheat" if they couldn't get there in time. Then there would be passing the parcel, and "Blind Man's Buff", and "pinning the tail on the donkey" whilst blindfolded, and charades, and "I spy", with occasional pauses for food, or helping Gran up to bed before it all got "too much" for her.

Gran was a frail, white-haired, tiny little person, who hardly ever talked because she found difficulty in breathing. She had an incessant dry cough, which wracked her scraggy shoulders. She stooped when she walked, which was only ever to the kitchen and back, and even then only by assisting herself, step-by-step, from the backs of chairs, to the door knob, and along the passage by way of the stair rails. Her cheekbones protruded and her cheeks were hollow; her face was the colour of polished ivory, and heavily wrinkled. She was never without a dish-cloth or a duster in her hand. She seemed to want to dust and clean and wash up, obsessively, as though to repay her daughter for being allowed to live with the family. She

130

wore a long pinafore down to her ankles, and her white hair was strained back from her bony face, and bunched like a tennis ball at the nape of her neck. When we called in on Sundays, after Sunday school, she would give George and me fourpence each, the price of entry to Bristol South swimming baths in Dean Lane. My mother loved her, and worried about her; but Gran seemed to display little affection in return. I could only hazard a guess at why Auntie Lottie, Gran's sister, had taken control of my mother's early life; I was never really sure.

My father was always a hit at the Boxing Day frivolities. He had a weird sense of humour, and never failed to make me laugh, even though I had seen and heard his antics so many times before. Some of his sayings were parodies of well-known phrases; so, "Procrastination is the Thief of Time", could become "respiration", or "assassination", or anything else which sprung to mind, as the "Thief of Time". Similarly, "Necessity is the Mother of Invention", could be transposed into "Bad feet are the Mother of Detention". I found this pricelessly funny, as I did when we got back from long family walks, and he would flop down on the doorstep and say, "I must sit down – your mother's feet are killing her!"

He could do an excellent clog-dance, until my mother laughingly told him to sit down and shut up, whereupon he would give his impression of a cowed husband, only too anxious to please a bullying wife, and stoop, and cringe, and tug his forelock. Uncle George was never sure how to respond to my father in these moods. He himself was the self-appointed life-and-soul-of-the-party. When he threw his head back and boomed out his laugh, everyone would dutifully laugh with him, and his broad smile would grow broader, and his double row of teeth would grow wider, and Christian jollity would ooze from the man. He was a nice person, but not the one I would want to be the keeper of my conscience, and I sensed that my father felt the same way.

I liked it best when the time came to sing. My father had a beautiful bass voice; Uncle Fred and he sang in the Shaftesbury Crusade Male Voice Choir, and my uncle had a splendidly high and sweet tenor. Uncle George had a robust and muscular baritone, which owed more to volume than to beauty. My mother's main role was to point out where we had gone wrong, and Auntie Harriet played a correct, Sunday-school type accompaniment on the piano.

The rest of us chipped in where we could. We all knew our place, and sometimes the resulting harmony could be very enjoyable.

Then we would pack up, and wend our way homewards, joining small groups of other, similar party-goers, walking back home. Without my father there to make a clown of himself in the interests of cheering us all up, there was no sparkle to Boxing Day celebrations that year. I took hold of the front wheels of the baby's pushchair to help my mother descend, one by one, the steps of Bartlett's Bridge, and wondered yet again why there had to be a war, and how long it would last.

Uncle Fred was a large, happy man, with a big stomach and a high voice. He had a good job as an engineering worker, and was the same age as my father. I once asked my father why Uncle Fred was not in the army; and my father replied darkly that he had been wondering that himself, for ages. I guessed what he meant, but we wouldn't dream of letting my mother know how we felt. She was devoted to her younger sister, even if there was little sign of her feelings being reciprocated. Eventually, Uncle Fred joined the Home Guard, and from the fuss he made you would think he had been asked to storm the Siegfried Line single-handed. When they sent him on exercises on Mendip one Saturday night in the summer, Auntie Jessie wept all the weekend, and welcomed him back for his Sunday lunch as though he had been a Dunkirk survivor. Next time he was sent away for the night, I was told to go and stay at her house, no doubt to take command, although her two sons (one older than me) and her daughter, were very much at home at the time.

On that occasion I had to stay until Monday morning, because my uncle, feeling a little jaded, had gone straight to bed. Consequently it was an extra long trudge for me to school that day, and I used the time to reflect on the ironies of life. My father was in the army, and we didn't know when, or if, we would ever see him again. My mother was struggling to bring up four small boys, and with precious little money to do so. I was supposed to take a leading role, at the age of ten, in helping my mother to keep things going. Yet here I was, walking to school from a different and distant direction, to accommodate my relations, who included one huge uncle with a good job but forced to spend an occasional weekend away from home; and three cousins, one of whom was two years older than me.

I had heard my Auntie Jessie anxiously asking my mother if she was happy about my attending a school like Merrywood. I had almost laughed out loud. I was now still only ten years old, but in my short recollection, I had moved house three times, been bombed out, re-housed, blitzed, sent away to Cornwall, and lived with two sets of complete strangers. At the same time my father had been taken away from us, and I had acquired two younger brothers as well as George, who was still only eight years old.

I had gained so much experience, so quickly, that I failed to see how anything could jolt me out of the private inner regime that I had secretly adopted.

24

That summer I remember learning several lessons. They had to do with "social awareness", if you wanted to play with words. Or you could call it snobbery, if you preferred to be brutally accurate. And they taught me that having a cut-glass accent is not always a sign of affluence, any more than coming from Bedminster is an indication of worthiness.

My mother had arranged a day out in Clevedon for us. We had been there, once, for a friend's Sunday school outing. I was fascinated with this gentle, dignified old town. The sea front wasn't much, and neither was the pier; but they didn't pretend to be anything, except a Victorian resort that knew how to grow old gracefully. I knew little about it beyond the walk from the railway station to the sea front, but on this visit my mother had a fancy to walk us all up Dial Hill before we went to the beach; she said the view from there across the channel was wonderful on a fine day. So she pushed Philip, my youngest brother, in his pushchair, and we all took the strain nobly on the handles, as the hill got steeper. She was quite fatigued when we reached the top, and she was a little disappointed with what she saw, so she marched us all back down the hill to find the beach. Unfortunately she didn't know the way, and she stopped and leaned against the handle of the pushchair while she recovered her breath and tried to get her bearings. She wished to avoid leading her small tribe round in circles to find the correct route by trial and error, and at that moment a lady emerged from a side road and walked towards us. "Ask that lady how to get to the seafront," she said to me. "And don't forget to say 'please!'." So I approached the lady and stopped politely. She was quite old, and a bit tubby, and wore a large green velvet hat with a big hat-pin. Her face was heavily made up, and she wore small spectacles from which dangled a black cord. She wore long clothes, and tan-coloured gloves, and green pointed shoes, which even I could guess were very expensive. She seemed to be gazing in the air at something, although I couldn't see anything that should be holding her attention so fixedly.

"Excuse me," I said, "Can you tell me the way to the sea front?" She obviously hadn't heard, because she walked steadily on, her eyes roving around the rooftops. I asked her again as she drew alongside, but she hurried past me without checking her stride, and left a trail of perfume in her wake. I turned to my mother.

"The lady didn't hear what I was saying," I explained. There could be no other reason for her failure to answer me. My mother's face was red and angry.

"Don't worry, son," she said quietly. "She heard you alright. But she didn't want to speak to you. She's My Lady of Clevedon!"

I can remember those very words, as clearly as though they were spoken yesterday. My mother made the remark with no malice at all, but I could see that she was deeply hurt. She even looked a bit disappointed that a lady could behave like that. It took me some time to realise that she was telling me that certain people would not wish to talk to a family like ours; and I couldn't see why. But I never forgot that incident.

And I contrasted it later with the bearing of little Miss Dukes. My father loved music, and as a surprise for him, my mother arranged for me to have piano lessons, optimistically expecting that I would be able to play a tune for him when he came home on his next leave. It sounded a grand idea when she broached it, and I wondered where on earth we would get the money for me to learn to play the piano. But, through one of her charlady jobs in Clifton, she had heard of a music teacher, Miss Dukes, who would visit you at your home and give lessons for a shilling an hour, provided she had a cup of tea before she left.

I don't know what I expected, but at the agreed time there was a knock on the door, and I opened it. On the doorstep was a tiny little lady, her back slightly bent with a deformity, and a radiant smile. She leant heavily on a walking stick, and carried a leather case in the other hand. She wore a simple navy-blue hat, a tweed coat buttoned all the way down; her eyes were as blue as the sky, and as mischievous as a young girl's. She was as thin as Albert Mills' whippet. She smiled at me, put her stick on the other arm, and shook hands with me.

"Good afternoon," she said politely, ignoring the scarlet blush which had suffused my face at the act of shaking hands with a lady. "I am Miss Dukes. I believe your mother is expecting me." My mother suddenly appeared from behind me, all flushed and skittish, and slightly embarrassed, and pleased as Punch to be talking to this lady.

135

"Come in," she said, and stood aside, her red apple cheeks glowing with pleasure. Miss Dukes thanked her, and her tiny figure limped across the small hallway, at the foot of the stairs. Even my mother was taller than she was. Her stick clacked upon the linoleum, and she went into our living room, saying all sorts of kind things about our house, although I knew it was not as nice as she was pretending. And yet I could sense that she was not being patronising; she was skilfully doing her best to break the ice. She chattered away happily in a very refined voice, and seemed intensely interested in everything my mother had to say. They went at it like old friends, right from the outset.

Miss Dukes had walked all the way from Hotwells, a distance of two or three miles, just to earn a shilling. And when she had had her cup of tea, she would walk all the way back, despite her age and her walking stick. She had a very superior accent, but she was such a lady; a real lady. She gave me my lesson on our old, out of tune piano, treating it carefully as though it were a Baby Grand and didn't sound like a barrel organ. She showed me the fingering, English and Continental, and named the notes, and made me play F.A.C.E. and C.A.B.B.A.G.E . Finally she gave me some work to practise and some "Theory" to do. Then she sat down, had her cup of tea and one of my mother's rock-cakes, and walked all the way back to Hotwells, thanking my mother profusely for her kindness, and promising to come on the same day next week. This, she said, was a genuine lady, and quite unlike the person we had been unfortunate enough to meet at Clevedon. Miss Dukes' family had once been well off, but now she was on her own, unmarried, and living in one room in Hotwells, near where she had been born and brought up. That fact alone must have made her feel very bitter, but you could never sense it. She made a frugal living by giving piano lessons in the area, and must have often looked back at her youth, and the big house, and the servants which her family undoubtedly employed. But never once did she let it be seen that her reduced circumstances bothered her. She steadfastly remained a lady, and consequently she was treated as a lady. She would never have turned me into a Paderewski, but she tried; and I admired her so much that I did my best to improve, just to please her. She passed away several months later, but I always hold her as an image of what a gentlewoman really was.

In case I was developing ideas that Bedminster folk were the salt of the earth, and could never be like My Lady of Clevedon in any possible way, events showed me very painfully that dreadful people could appear anywhere, and without any notice.

It was a hot afternoon in the summer holiday, a week or so after our experience in Clevedon, and I suddenly felt that what I wanted in life most of all at that moment, was a swim. The day stands out prominently in my recollection still because I couldn't find my swimming costume, and my mother was out. Determination is no doubt an excellent quality, but it can be a fearsome slave driver. All that stood between a swim and me was the lack of a costume. Therefore I must produce a costume from somewhere. I decided I could make one. I took one of my mother's large dish cloths out of the drawer, hunted up her sewing scissors, and cut the cloth into two equal shapes which I reckoned would do as the front and the back of a pair of swimming trunks. I then did the most forbidden thing one could do in our house; I opened up my mother's sewing machine and tried to use it. After all, what was necessary was only the stitching of the front to the back, and I would have a serviceable pair of trunks. I couldn't fill the bobbin with cotton, couldn't thread the needle, and could scarcely make the wheel turn, even by stamping as hard as I could upon the treadle.

At this point my mother came home and caught me red-handed. Of course, I should have realised how precious that sewing machine was to her. Not only did it keep our clothes neat and tidy in my mother's expert hands; it had many times been the only means of earning some money when money was very badly needed, and my mother took in some sewing. She had not been so cross with me for years, and yet she understood that I was not being wicked; I was just as determined as she was, and was intent on making a pair of swimming trunks. She found my trunks, like mothers do when others lose things, within about five seconds of looking, and told me to get out of her sight and enjoy my swim. So off I went, much chastened, and with my Gran's swimming bath money in my pocket.

Dean Lane Baths was a modern looking, red-brick building, built between the wars. You climbed several steps to the entrance, and walked inside, in the comparative gloom, to the pay-desk. The lady, who may possibly once have been smiling and cheerful, was none of that now. Had she ever possessed any Christian charity, it had been efficiently eroded by years of sitting at the kiosk and dealing with the spirited youth of Bedminster.

You entered the pool itself through a double-door, and the first sensation was of warm, strong chemicals in the air. My mother said it was chlorine, on the days I came home with my eyes red and itching. At the far end of the pool was a diving stage, with confident divers springing off the lower boards, and terrified experimentalists perched on the top stage, shivering, knees bent and arms crossed over chests, trying hard to find the courage to leap. The changing cubicles had canvas draw-curtains, and flanked the pool down both sides. Proceedings were under the supervision of a baths attendant, with a whistle on a cord hanging from his neck, and wearing a white shirt and a pair of cricket flannels. Tucked in behind the diving boards was a shallow, rectangular pool designed for feet washing before swimming. This unhygienic area was the main "swimming" pool for timid youngsters, of whom I had been one until fairly recently.

But the main impression as you opened the door was the noise. Bathers shouted, boys yelled as they dive-bombed screaming girls, the attendant's whistle blew incessantly as he attempted to correct miscreants from the side of the pool and received hearty derision in return. Divers splashed, spring-boards shuddered, and the air was filled with such an instant and high level of noise that you could have stepped straight out of Dean Lane into a frightening underworld.

All the changing-booths around the pool were occupied that afternoon, and the supervisor had opened the large competitors' changing-room at the side, to take the overflow. Everyone changed together, hanging their clothes on a single peg if they could find one free. In the pool the noise, as usual, was deafening. The attendant, with powers not visited on ordinary mortals, could apparently judge when you had been in the pool for your allotted half an hour, whereupon he would blow his whistle, point at you, and say "Out!" Some of the lads grew suddenly very hard of hearing at this juncture, and swam to the far corners of the baths, and had to be individually harried by the furious official. What with the screaming and the whistling, and the shouting, and the denials of the transgressors, there was a state of permanent pandemonium, and I was quite glad when my time was up.

I climbed out of the pool, made my way over the wet tiles, dodged around the streaming presence of other swimmers, and into the changing room. I found my clothes peg; but that was about all I ever found. Except for my trousers, all the clothes I had arrived in, were missing. My shoes and socks had gone from under the bench, and so had my towel, shirt, and pullover. The thief had kindly left me my trousers, and that was all. I was shocked, and I had a good look around in case I had made a mistake, or perhaps somebody had shifted them to make way for his own. Deep down, I knew they had been stolen; but I also knew there was no point in panicking. With a crowded pool and an overflowing changing room, it was unlikely that I could ask anybody if they had seen my kit with any likelihood of success. I had been robbed, and now I must think my way out of the situation.

I am ashamed to say that I was angry as well as upset, and it did actually cross my mind to look along the rows of pegs and see if I could select some replacement clothing when nobody was looking. It could even be that someone else had been robbed, and had done just that to me. But I dismissed the idea without even considering the repercussions when I got home. Instead, I put on my trousers, went to the lady at the cash desk, and put myself at her mercy. She sucked her teeth a bit, as though I was asking the impossible. Then she reached under the desk and handed me the old pair of suede shoes she used for shuffling about on the wet floors. Then she went into the lost property cupboard and came back with a Fair Isle pullover, which smelt very musty and which just about fitted. She was very sorry, but that was the best she could do, and I thanked her and hurried out, down the steps into Dean Lane. I heard her shouting "Bring they shoes back, mind!" and I shouted back that I would.

I was wearing women's shoes, my own trousers, an old pullover, and carrying my wet costume. I was also feeling bitterly resentful at whoever had robbed me, but had the common sense to think a little before I did anything. I considered my options, and decided that I could not possibly walk to Lynton Road in this outfit; so I turned right and walked up British Road, where my Aunty Jessie lived. She was marvellous. She immediately found some clothes belonging to my cousins, gave me a glass of lemonade and a slice of cake, and I was ready to go home. "I'd better take those shoes back to the lady at the Baths," I said.

"Too late now," she replied; "They're in the dustbin, along with that dirty old pullover. Off you go and tell your mother."

I walked home, and concluded, in the sage way that ten-year-olds sometimes have, that there was more than one kind of wickedness in the world. My Lady of Clevedon had wounded my mother without saying a word. Miss Dukes had been badly treated by the world in general, but never for a second showed any resentment. And I had been robbed and humiliated; but at least my pride had been saved, and the clothes I had from my cousins were better than the gear I had lost. I reckoned it wasn't so much the calamity that mattered, but how you dealt with it.

I must have been right, because when I got home and tried to explain my reasoning to my mother, she promptly agreed.

25

My father arrived home on leave, suddenly and unexpectedly. Once again it was "Embarkation leave", but this time he had a rough idea of where he was going next. "We're going to France, or Belgium," he said, carelessly including both countries as easily as if he was proposing a walk to Long Ashton. He reached into his kit bag and produced a French information handbook which the army had issued to all troops, to help them understand the French and their language. My mother had forgotten all the French she knew, and I had never even heard it spoken; but I was quite sure that our Allies over the Channel would have been very alarmed if they could hear the way my father was steadily murdering their language, and was about to invade their shores. Compared to him, "Monsewer" Eddie Gray sounded like a French aristocrat.

We were still kept short of hard news, but the carefully prepared bulletins that reached us on the wireless were now boundlessly optimistic. Mr. Churchill no longer needed to stiffen the backs of the people at home with his wonderful rallying speeches. It was now deemed safe to allow us to go to Scout camps for a weekend, and we thoroughly enjoyed ourselves, under Ern's enthusiastic direction, at such mysterious wilderness redoubts as Flax Bourton, Stanton Drew, and Penpole Point.

There were never any cars parked in the street, so we played cricket up against our front gate, where we had chalked three stumps. If a vehicle had lost its way and trundled accidentally up Lynton Road we all shouted, "Car!" and stopped playing for a moment to allow the motor through, stooping to see if we could recognise the driver as he passed. Otherwise, the only impediment to our game was the odd bicycle, propped up on the kerb by its pedals; and this could easily be moved away from the playing area. We used a bat, sawn out of a plank and sandpapered around the handle; and a tennis ball. The pull to square-leg and the cut to point were the only strokes which would propel the ball any distance up or down the street. It you struck it straight, you hit the privet hedges, and you couldn't run because you had to find it yourself. If you hit it into a garden three times, you were out. "Three gardeners and you're out!" unknown at the M.C.C., was one of our most rigid rules. The lbw rule was applied often, but regularly ignored. Bisto Smith, in a lifetime of street cricket, was never once out lbw. Neither was he ever bowled, because he always disputed the spot where the ball hit the gate; and he was only caught when it was so obvious that even he couldn't argue. He just refused to go.

Some neighbours were anti-street games; others were anti-any games we played. During that winter we made a glorious slider on a frosty pavement. We queued up to run onto it and gingerly allowed ourselves to glide ten yards or so to the end. Then you ran to the back of the queue and did it again. When the man next door to Mr. Andrews saw it, he went in, and came out with a large lump of salt, which he threw down on the ice and it melted. As it turned into water, we shouted indignantly at him, but he only shrugged his reply. "Too bloody dangerous," he said, and went back indoors.

We also had some exhilarating "Charges" against the Knowle-Westers who lived at the top of the Novers. At regular intervals, and for no apparent reason, a "Charge" would suddenly develop. The word went around Lynton Road like lightning that the kids from Knowle West were ready for a fight. We would raid the streets for dustbin lids, rally friends into the army, fill our pockets with stones, and line up to repel the mob from up the hill. The dustbin lids were meant to be shields, but it was difficult to throw stones and protect your head simultaneously, and I once collected a severe gash on the forehead. I went home to have it dressed, but my mother said that our gang could fight quite well without me, so I watched from the bedroom window as the battle was brought to a dramatic halt when we launched our secret weapon. One of the boys had an elder brother who owned an air pistol, and actually had some lead pellets. All he had to do was to advance on the Knowle-Westers, gun arm extended, and they fled in terror. Agincourt had nothing on us.

We all knew secret "knackies", places where the best bluebells grew, or primroses, or cowslips, and we would take them home by the armful, in spite of the fact that they would be half dead on arrival owing to lack of water. As the year progressed we went from flowers to crab apples, blackberries, conkers and chestnuts, and even hazel nuts, with their russet kernels and thick leaves. We knew where there were springs of pure water, and planned our sorties up

142

to Dundry and back, so that, like desert travellers, we could stop at waterholes and fill up our bottles.

The Malago and the Novers, and the slopes up to Dundry, were sufficient to satisfy our desire for adventure. There were dens to be dug and fires to be lit, taking care always, when you built a stove, not to use stones from the stream; they were apt to explode. You selected potatoes which weren't too large from your mother's kitchen, and pushed a twig into them, and left them in the red ashes, turning them carefully until they were black and the skins were crisp. Baked potatoes were something to be dreamed of.

We had long become accustomed to the tall wooden posts, like pit props, sunk into the ground where the meadows widened. My father said these were to stop enemy gliders from landing. The area was dotted with redbrick square blocks, with slits left open for rifle fire. These were mostly pointed to shoot down country roads; many roads had holes excavated in them and filled in lightly, so that concrete blocks could be thrust into place if the tanks tried to advance. And it always delighted me to see squads of soldiers on the march, more or less in step, unless it was a ceremonial occasion. If that was the case, the ranks and files would be ruler-straight, the rifles all pointed to the sky at exactly the same angle, knuckles would point stiffly at the right shoulder of the man in front, and the NCO in charge would study his platoon like a circling fox. But it was not yet time for very much in the way of military ceremonials.

Evenings went on and on, because of Double British Summer-time. We went to bed in the daylight, and read, or listened to ITMA, or the Big Bands, or any one of a stream of comedians and singers and acts like "We Three from Happidrome". Many of the performers were under the direction of something called "ENSA". I asked my father what that stood for, and he said "Every Night, Something Awful." But he said it with a laugh, so I didn't believe him.

His leave seemed to be over before it began, but there was a certain lightheartedness in the air this time. We knew that now he really was going abroad, and would certainly be in more danger in Europe than he had been in the Shetland Islands. Perhaps we had got used to his being away. Although we loved him as much as ever, it had been a year since we last saw him, and a year in the life of a ten-year-old is a long time. But my mother was thrilled to have him

143

to herself, and my two young brothers, who barely remembered him, at last were allowed to see for themselves what their father actually looked like. He was forever talking about "demobilisation", about the order in which soldiers would be allowed to leave the army. They looked at your age, the size of your family, and no doubt many other factors, and worked out your number from that. When your time came, everybody in your group would be released at the same time. But those were only the plans; the end of the war was still a long way off, and nobody had yet been given a number; and there was always the war against Japan to think of.

My father packed his gear, and once again there was sadness in the air as he looked glumly at us, gave us a manly hug, kissed my mother, and disappeared for another year or more. Life would turn a few more bewildering circles before he returned.

26

And so the summer of 1944 drew to its close. Air raids were a thing of the past. Rationing was still very much in force, but nuisances like blackout curtains and sleeping in air raid shelters were way behind us. The war, to everyone's eyes, was all but won, and notices were appearing, usually painted on walls, in the dark, urging Mr. Churchill to "Open the Second Front Now". Personally I didn't much care what the Second Front was. My father was in France, or Belgium, and it would still be a long time before we could welcome him back to the family. There was also, although we never mentioned it, still time for him to be lost in action and not come back at all.

But for the moment, I was preoccupied with preparations for starting my spell at Merrywood Grammar School for Boys, Headmaster A. E. Jones, Esq., M.A. (Oxon.) I had already revelled in a privilege the boys who went to Marksbury Road School didn't enjoy. Merrywood's holidays were not in line with the rest, and we had a couple of days extra before we were due to register. There was a very scrupulous "School Board" at the time, in the form of a middle-aged gentleman in a trilby who rode his bicycle around the area, looking for lads who ought to be at school but had declined to attend. Officially they would be playing truant, although we had several more descriptive names for this syndrome. I used to wait for this man; you could see him at the far end of the road, wobbling towards you on his bike, with a raincoat strapped to his handlebars, eager to catch a miscreant. I, on the other hand, was just as eager to be caught, so that I could announce with great indifference, that "I was a Merrywood boy", and thus immune from his petty regulations.

This pleased me immensely, but didn't cheer him up at all. There was nothing he could do, but he threatened that if he ever caught me out of school when I should be in, I was in for a large slice of trouble, for my cheek.

But now it was mid-September, and time to go, and I was ready early. All new boys had received a note concerning expected standards of uniform. The well-dressed boy would have a cap, a tie, a blazer or blazer badge, a scarf, socks, and a satchel. The school had sent us a list, saying all these could be obtained at "Smart-wear", in East Street, Bedminster. There were also details of the requisite sports gear, including the school football jersey, without which no boy could expect to play for the school. As usual, I resigned myself to acquiring the minimum equipment, at the least expense. Thankfully, there was not an envious bone in my body; what other people could afford never bothered me in the slightest. On the other hand, the minimum had to be achieved somehow. I picked blackberries at 6 a.m. in Leigh Woods, and sold them to greengrocers in North Street before 8.30. I collected jam jars and scrap metal, and sold it in the Red Cow Yard in West Street, and with the money I went a few yards down to Polly Reynold's second-hand shop, and bought what I thought was suitable, fortified by the religious tracts she handed out to customers.

With a cap, a tie, my own jacket, and an old music case for a satchel, I walked down Lynton Road towards Parson Street, with my mother's good luck kiss stinging in my ears because I hadn't ducked quickly enough. Nobody else was approaching the school from my direction, but there was a stream of pupils coming down Parson Street and starting the very long climb up the steps to the rear entrance. I knew that the main entrance was in Downton Road, on the Knowle West side of the school, and that would be even busier. There were as many girls as boys, but nowhere did boys and girls walk together. Many had bikes, and pushed them up the steps. They all seemed to have bulky leather or brown canvas satchels, and I wondered what they were carrying in them to make them look so full.

The flow of pupils narrowed at a gate at the top, to admit them in twos and threes, at which the girls swung off to the right, and the boys went straight ahead. To our right was the girls' gymnasium, and I quickly heard the murmur that, if you as much as glanced at the window, it meant the cane for you at once. The crocodile continued past another gymnasium, this time the boys' building; and I realised that the boys' school and the girls' school were mirror images of each other in the size and layout. But to even look towards the girls' section was as forbidden as wandering into a leper colony. I found no problem with that, however.

We turned right into a small yard, where the boys with bicycles locked them in bicycle sheds, taking their pumps and lamps off first.

Then we waited around the front entrance until a big boy, a prefect, no less, signalled that we should come in. Three hundred-plus boys stampeded into the cloakrooms, along the corridors, and lined up for Assembly in the main hall. The masters lined one wall, seated on chairs, and the boys stood in orderly ranks according to which form they belonged to. The new boys were called "fags", and stood in the front. A boy sat at the piano and played tunes until the Headmaster and his deputy appeared, whereupon the teachers stood up and Mr. Jones flowed in. He wore a gown, as did all the teachers, but his seemed to be longer and billowed more. Beneath it he wore a pinstriped suit and waistcoat, and he walked leaning backwards, with his feet splayed out, like a penguin. He was plump and bald, and his skin was puffy and unhealthy. His forehead was corrugated with thick wrinkles. He nodded kindly at certain of the masters, some of whom I thought were ready to bow to him, although he seemed to be enjoy it.

He said a few words, announced the hymn, and his deputy, Mr. Gay, read a brief lesson. Then he gave a short welcome to all pupils returning for another year at Merrywood, and an even shorter acknowledgement of the fact that there were 60 or 70 new boys present, and would they stay behind. Then he floated off again, looking straight ahead, eyebrows raised, a slack half-smile on his face. No wonder they called him "Slug". Mr. Gay followed, beaming at the ceiling, and sundry heads bobbed amongst the teaching staff as they passed. The boy on the piano struck up a Percy Grainger tune, and the boys shuffled quietly back to their classrooms. We in the front few ranks were left gazing at each other and wondering what the next move would be.

A master appeared, carrying a big ledger. He dressed rather sharply for a teacher. His hair was short but not like a soldier's; his eyes were narrowed and he had a large nose. He spoke through a constant, pitying grin at us. His name was Mr. Kerr. He looked at us sadly, and shook his head. "Five per cent," he said; "You lot are supposed to represent the top five per cent of the intellect at your age in this fair city of ours." He shrugged his shoulders in resignation. "Sit down!" he ordered, and we slithered, crossed legged, to the floor, while he propped his back against the front of the stage and consulted his book. He called out our names, and looked at us, one by one, disbelievingly. We, in turn, found some amusement in some of the names he read out. "Hector Johnson," he intoned; and somebody repeated, "Hector!" and sniggered. "Roderick Hannay," he continued, and the boy behind me said "Bloody Hell!", and several more boys guffawed. I was intrigued to hear my friend Bob Flower's name when it was called.

"Francis William Robert Flower," said Mr. Kerr, the master. "That's a good set of names, Flower?" I settled back to watch the inevitable conflict; I knew he would never intimidate Bob.

"We'm all called Francis William in our family, Sir," he explained innocently, "Except for the last name, which you chooses yerself!" I recognised the bogus Bristol accent at once, and mentally wished Mr. Kerr the best of luck.

"All of you?" sneered Mr. Kerr.

"Not the girls, Sir. My sisters is called . . ."

"That will do, Flower," said Mr. Kerr, retreating because he was

148

approaching thin ice and sensed that he was being lured onto it by an eleven-year old boy.

The name "Llewellyn Osmond" got a good laugh, especially when the owner blushed bright pink at the revelation.

"Welsh, are you, Osmond?" said a more heroic Mr. Kerr, happier to be on firmer ground against a lesser foe.

"No, Sir," piped up Osmond, in a strangely high voice for such a tall lad. "Winford, Sir. I come on the country bus, Sir." Mr. Kerr was not impressed by this gratuitous piece of information. When Fowler and Chapman said "So do I, Sir," in unison, he shouted at them to shut up. Maurice Marks was there, grinning as usual, and received a searing stare from Mr. Kerr for his trouble. Having checked us all in, he wanted to know our fathers' occupations. What on earth this had to do with our education, I shall never know. Bob Flower and I said our fathers were in the army.

"And what did they do before that?" enquired the supercilious Mr. Kerr. I didn't want to say "road sweeper" in this august company, and Bob was not proposing to reveal that his dad had been a lorry driver. So I said that my father worked for the Transport and Cleansing Dept. of Bristol Corporation, which was true; and Bob confided that his dad was a transport executive. He justified this to me later by saying that on Saturday mornings, when the boss didn't come in, his dad was deputy foreman. I heartily agreed that this did indeed make him a transport executive.

Mr. Kerr then led us to our classrooms. In the first year we were grouped alphabetically, so we found ourselves seated in more-or-less alphabetical order. We copied our timetables from the blackboard, were told the School Rules (don't run – walk; keep off the grass; obey the prefects, etc.) and were told how much our books would cost. We met our Form Master, Mr. Aulman, who would also teach us French. He was shaped like a crow with his gown on; slightly bent from the shoulders, glasses perched on a pointed nose, sparse shiny hair across the top of his scalp, and a cutting tongue. He stood no nonsense, but I liked him.

And we spent the rest of the morning finding our way around and filling in forms, an occupation without which no establishment can hope to survive.

149

27

Suddenly, my first morning at Merrywood Grammar School for Boys was over, and the bells rang like a fire alarm. I joined the rush out into the yard, scaled the fence of the playing field that ringed the boys' half of the school, and within minutes was plunging down our back path and into the kitchen.

"How was it, then?" mother asked keenly, wiping her hands on a dishcloth.

"Not bad," I said.

I was famished, but knew I would get no food unless I was a little more forthcoming than that.

"Pretty good, really," I continued hurriedly. "The teachers all wear gowns. They've got a big gymnasium, with showers, and a Physics Lab., and a Chemistry Lab., and an Art Room, and a Library. You've got to keep off the grass, and not even look at the girls; and you've got to behave yourself, otherwise the teachers and the prefects will have you. I've got to be back in the Quadrangle in forty minutes." This was a prompt to my mother. Didn't she realise that her starving Young Hero needed some attention?

"Did you know anybody there?" she asked. I reached at last for my knife and fork.

"I saw General going up the steps," I said helpfully.

"Who on earth is General?" demanded my mother.

"Beryl Waycott," I replied. "And Bob Flower was there, and Maurice Marks, and other some kids from Victoria Park School."

I told her about Assembly, and the discipline, and murals on the wall at the main entrance. I threw in every tit-bit which I thought might interest her, and then reached for my jacket.

"What are you doing this afternoon?" she queried; "I've got your list here." But I was away up over the Novers, to make my dent on the seat of learning which would be mine for the next five years at least.

Had I cared to wait and look at my mother's schedule, it would have been obvious that the next session was football "– in the playground, on this occasion." And I brought no kit whatsoever. But I was determined to play, so I said that although I was usually a

150

half-back, I could also play very well in goal. I said this because I had observed that everyone was fighting not to be goalie, so at least there would be no opposition. Alan Locke, who was a keen but not very talented footballer, assumed control of affairs. He and his pal John Chivers came from Ashton, and what Lockie didn't know, Chivers did, so we were in no danger of running out of ideas. Lockie designated me as goalie, although it was nothing to do with him really. I was wearing my only pair of shoes, knowing that I would be in trouble with my mother when I got home if she knew I had used them to play football. On the way back down the Novers that evening I stopped, sat down, took them off, and gave them a good scrubbing with spit and long grass. They passed muster; or at least, my mother made no remark, which was not always the same thing. You had to be cute to deceive my mother for long. When I went to bed that night, she said perhaps I would consider using my sports kit next time, so I knew that she had not been fooled after all; she was just making allowances because it was my first day at school.

That first week flew by, but not without teaching me some lessons about how the approach of masters could differ in terms of keeping order. One day, in fact, was enough to destroy my interest in mathematics forever. At Victoria Park School I had been rather good at the subject. I much preferred English, and History and the rest, but, after all, when I left I had been top of the school in arithmetic. We were doing maths under the tutelage of a small, bald-headed master, with a big nose and gold-rimmed spectacles. His face had a perpetual sneer, and his style was to bully and be sarcastic, and generally behave as though the class comprised congenital idiots for whom there was no hope on this earth. We were doing compound interest, and I raised my hand to ask a question.

"Yes?" he barked impatiently, as though I was intruding on a lecture by Euclid.

"Sir," I said politely, "In my last school we did that in a slightly different way."

He rushed over to me, and examined me closely to see if I had gone dangerously insane.

"*What* did you say?" he demanded incredulously, as though I had blasphemed aloud in Westminster Abbey. I repeated it courteously, whereupon his face suddenly caught fire, and he clutched his gown tightly at the neck with both fists.

"While you are in this school, boy, you will learn mathematics in the way that I tell you, and nobody else." And he slapped me hard across the face.

I was astonished. He had not so much hurt me, as humiliate me, in front of a bunch of strange classmates. That was the last question I ever remember asking in a maths lesson. From then on I hated the subject; and yet, moments earlier, I had been as keen as anyone to learn. Boys quickly sense the atmosphere in a classroom; they can tell fair play from unfairness quicker than a master. They can rapidly differentiate between clowns who get what they deserve, from those who are being unjustly treated. When the master returned to the blackboard, everyone was sullen. No questions were asked, and nobody was interested any more. This was not fair dealing, and they all knew it. And fair play counts as highly as not telling tales in a schoolboy's judgement.

Later in the term, Mr. Mair, the English master, who was liked and respected by everyone, hurt me also, but quite inadvertently. Personally, I revered him, which made me easier to upset. But I was quite happy that he was acting fairly, and when the rest of the class laughed I knew they were laughing at the situation and not at me.

We were reading Shakespeare's *The Merchant of Venice*, and Mr. Mair had given each of us a part to take and read aloud, like a play in rehearsal. I was given the part of Shylock, and I was intensely interested. Mr. Mair had explained the plot, and pointed out that it revolved around the moneylender and his "bond", the security for his loan. I was so keen that I took the book home to study, and actually had the whole of the most important speech off by heart. It was the part when Salerio asks Shylock why he wants a pound of flesh. Shylock replies,

"To bait fish, withal. If t'will feed nothing else, t'will feed my revenge!"

I spent hours learning it. I could do the accents, and mime the actions. I was about to be a new Laurence Olivier, and all the class knew it and were highly amused. We all took our places, and waited for Mr. Mair to arrive.

He bustled in, a short, slim, middle-aged man, with receding sandy hair, and common-sense air about him. He was a skilful user of the English language, and could demolish you in one sentence. But he was never cruel. He went straight to the desk, and opened his *Merchant of Venice*.

"Right!" he said crisply, "Now we come to the important part. In fact, it is so important to the play, that I will read the part of "Shylock" myself. You don't mind, do you, Budd?"

The class roared with laughter, and Mr. Mair looked up in surprise. He sensed that something unusual had happened.

"You don't mind, do you, Budd?" he repeated, and then someone enlightened him. He saw the funny side more clearly than I did. But he was a fair man, and at least tried to explain why it was so important that he read the part of Shylock to us. I didn't so much give in, as make the most of the situation. But I knew Alec Mair was above all an honest man, and soon I was laughing as he asked me from time to time, if I thought he was doing quite well, and should he continue. Afterwards he told everyone not to be so clever, because I had set them an example and they should be grateful. They weren't of course; but honour was satisfied, and that was precisely what Mr. Mair, a teacher as well as a master, sought to achieve.

Merrywood was far from being a brutal school to attend; probably the local Secondary Modern Schools, Connaught Road and Marksbury Road, were even keener on thumping the boys. After all, these schools drew from a close catchment area of pretty tough people, whereas Merrywood drew pupils from a far larger range. Apart from the occasional whacking from "Slug" when groups of us made merry at the same time, I can only remember isolated instances in my first year when boys were punished unfairly.

The gymnasium was run by an ex-Bristol City footballer, a Scotsman whom they said was quite tough as a player. He was now large and balding, and gave most of his instructions from a wooden chair. He kept a "slipper", an old gym shoe, in his cupboard. His method of physical punishment was quite simple. If you erred, he chose another pupil to give you a whack across the backside while you bent over to receive it. If, however, the gym master thought the wielder of the slipper was not being whole-hearted about his job, he would call on a *third* boy to give the second boy a whacking, until the job was completed to his own satisfaction. We didn't respect this form of justice; there was something unfair about it, so it did nothing to make us repent, but just made us simmer, and dislike the old footballer.

Mr. Wilshire ("Without a T", he always insisted) was another matter. He was a science master, but he looked after football and cricket. He had played both games himself, and his keenness and dedication drove generations of Merrywood boys to ever-increasing heights of achievement. If you let "Wimpey" down, you were being unfair to him. His temperament could be erratic, but generally speaking he was very popular and highly respected.

One morning, he was giving us a lesson about combustible gases. He said that carbon dioxide was not combustible, and did not support combustion. I found this very puzzling, because every morning of my life, before breakfast, it was my job at home to clear the ashes out of the fire grate, clean it, and start a new fire. When it didn't burn quickly enough I stood the poker upright against the fire-bars, and spread a newspaper over it, tightly, to create a draught and speed up the process. When this didn't work, and I knew that time was flying, I put my face close to the embers and blew with all my might. This inevitably caused the fire to flare up immediately. I was blowing carbon dioxide into the fire. Carbon dioxide did not burn, or support combustion, so why did the fire flare up? Intensely interested in this phenomenon I raised my hand at once, and asked Mr. Wiltshire the question. To my utter astonishment, he flew into a rage, and gave me a mighty whack about the ears. I can still see him, a powerful, stocky man, with a big nose with a wart on one side, China-blue eyes, fair hair, and his face as scarlet as a pillar box. He was furious with me. I liked him immensely, but he had almost removed my head from my shoulders for asking what I thought was an intelligent question. Boys were now becoming very selective, not only about the questions they asked, but about to which master they should direct the question. This went right against Mr. Taylor's oft-repeated mantra, that if you did not question everything you would learn nothing.

The deputy Headmaster was Henry Gay. He was probably the oldest teacher in the school, and he was a man of immense dignity, even if he did usually fail to recognise his own pupils when he met them off the premises. He was slight, with closely cut grey hair, a rather large nose, and had a flat-footed way of walking. Mr. Gay could teach things you would never find in a textbook. He was in the army in Africa in the Great War, and thrilled us with his reminiscences. He told us, if you walked through the jungle and stepped on a certain insect, you would get "Chigga", and your foot would swell up. He had it once, and his African Orderly looked at Mr. Gay's foot, said "Chigga, bwana", and took out a knife to remove the insect before it could do any more damage. He knew about First Aid, and the bloodiest bits of the Bible, and what a scourge Communism was because its aim was to achieve equality by lowering standards for everybody, rather than teaching people to aim upwards. He could recite Rudyard Kipling by the mile, and he was the cause of my learning "If" and "The Road to Mandalay" off by heart, so that I could recite it to myself when I felt like it. His brother was the famous Bristol cleric, the Rev'd. Canon Percy Gay, of St. George's, Brandon Hill. He said his family came from Barnstaple, in Devon, and one of his ancestors was John Gay, who wrote *The Beggar's Opera*. I know we looked forward immensely to the spare periods, when he brought in his book of Devon country tales, headed *A Parcel of Ol' Crams*, by Jan Stewer. I must confess that, after living in Cornwall as an evacuee, I couldn't exactly trace the accent he used for Jan Stewer; but it was hilarious, nevertheless.

We respected his ability to bolster our academic education with chunks of real-life philosophy, but even he had a malicious streak, which flawed him in our eyes. It showed itself to the class when I was desperate to use the toilet, but he flatly refused to let me be "excused". I asked him several times, and he grew aggressive and threatened me about what would happen if I asked again. So I simply fled to the toilets without asking him, a pretty brave move for a boy in his first year when under orders from the deputy Head-master. I was only just in time to save a calamity, and on the way back I wondered what Mr. Gay had in store for me by way of punishment. But he had scented that indefinable atmosphere in the classroom, where nothing is said but everyone gets the point. He called me over, and solicitously asked me if I felt better, and what had I eaten for breakfast. He didn't fool me, or my classmates, but we all played along with him. He knew he was being unjust, and he knew that we knew it, and his vast experience of boys told him that his best move now was to do nothing.

It was Mr. Gay who committed one of the worst acts of unjustified punishment that I ever saw at school. Even a careful system of selection for boys to attend a grammar school could allow one or two poor fish to slip through the net. We had one of these in our class. He sat right at the front so that teachers had him under close watch. He was big and rough; he could be quite likeable, but only a few like him actually chose to have him as a friend. It was almost impossible for any master to persuade him to learn something. He was disruptive, never turned up to do "Detentions", and laughed at the cane. Mr. Gay was teaching us geography, and for some reason we saw that he had attracted this boy's interest to an astonishing level. The session continued after lunch, and the lad said he had a book at home with all that stuff in, and he was going to rush home during the lunch-break and bring it back for the afternoon lesson.

We doubted it, but well in time for the lesson, there he was, sitting at his desk, the book open at the appropriate page, pointing things out to a clutch of his flabbergasted cronies. The door opened, and Mr. Gay strode in. The boy looked up, like a puppy overjoyed to see his master. Friendliness and the desire to co-operate simply oozed from his countenance.

"Sir," he began. And that was as far as Mr. Gay let him go. Clutching the wrist of one hand with the palm of the other, he swung his arm and gave the boy a blow that would have stunned a horse. The boy couldn't believe it.

"Sir?" he said again, and received an even harder blow for his efforts. That did it. The boy rose to his feet and leaned towards Mr. Gay, holding the end of his desk.

"Hit me again," he invited. "Go on – hit me again."

Mr. Gay was frightened; I was sitting a yard away, and could see and hear it all. He stepped one pace backwards, and said aloud, but to himself, "What's he going to do?"

Then forty years of teaching experience came to his rescue, like a dazed boxer fighting on by instinct. "Go and stand over there," he said, pointing at the wall. He moved cautiously back to allow the boy to pass, pretending to ignore the glare of sheer hatred which he received on the way. Once again the class knew they had just witnessed something, not only cruel, but also unfair and unjust. Not only that, whatever love the boy would have possessed for learning, and any loyalty he felt for his school, was now smashed out of him for ever. Mr. Gay said "Read your books", and, when the bell rang,

156

he got up and swiftly disappeared, leaving us all sullen and resentful, and in no mood to be taught for the rest of the day.

Apart from these incidents, over which I pondered for a long time in reflective moments, my first term at school was increasingly enjoyable. But whatever I learnt, in between games, Gym and the rapidly growing friendship with my new schoolmates, I was already learning a deeper lesson. I quickly understood that life would never be really fair, although sometimes it went in your favour when you didn't deserve it. I decided that good work was not automatically rewarded, and that some kind men could be hurtful to you unwittingly. There were others who undoubtedly enjoyed hurting small boys. I never actually said, "Never explain; never complain." But I rapidly acquired an ability, born of the terribly disjointed life I had led so far, to learn the rules, accept them, bend them a little if necessary, and try not to hurt others in the process. I was able to remain silent, and observe, and learn. And I always felt most comfortable in my own company anyway.

But the discouragement shown by some masters to boys wanting to ask questions manifested itself in another way, which I found very disconcerting. The whole school were assembled one afternoon to hear a talk by police sergeant Locke, on the matter of Road Safety. Some of the statements he made were quite provocative. For instance, he said, "there is no such thing as an accident." When he finished, he asked for questions. Only one boy, "Prongs" Parker, asked a question. For the rest, over three hundred of us, there was silence. I knew the boys were interested. Did they really have no questions, or was "questioning" not part of the ethos of this school?

28
It took some time for me to make the transition from being a pupil of a junior school in Bedminster, to being an inmate of Merrywood Grammar School for Boys. The problem was not one for me; it was Bisto Smith and his gang who couldn't come to grips with the situation. I thought this was a great shame, because usually I got on very well with the lads in the street. I could play cricket and football as well as they could, and was an enthusiastic participant in any devilry which was afoot. But the moment I put on my cap and went out with my case of homework, I apparently represented something alien to Lynton Road. I became a "Merrywood Sissy". Sometimes there was no problem; but, too often, I found my cap being pulled off and thrown from hand to hand, my case thrown over the privet hedge, and my tie used to garrotte me. When I came home from school in the afternoons, I was ambushed more times than Davey Crockett.

I didn't take it lying down. If there were only one or two, I could usually handle them, but it only took a catalyst for real trouble to begin. That catalyst was invariably Bisto Smith, and one day he went too far. I realised that if I didn't do something drastic now, this torment could go on for ages. The turning point came when I was on the way home from school with a model windmill, which had just won me first prize in a school model-making competition. My mother and I had worked all night on that windmill, and it not only looked good, but it actually worked. The sails would turn realistically at the slightest touch, the doors and windows opened, and there was even a spindle and a handle for winding up sacks of corn.

I was hurrying home with this trophy as quickly as I could, because I couldn't wait to tell my mother that our joint efforts had won the prize. Suddenly, Bisto Smith ran up behind me, snatched it from me, and threw it to Ginger Williams. In less than a minute it had been reduced to a handful of shredded paper and cardboard, and I knew the time had come to make a stand.

Yorath Davies was our expert on boxing. He had to be, because he said that his dad had once knocked out Tommy Farr when they

158

lived in Tonypandy, so naturally his word on fighting was final. He said that Bisto Smith and I should fight things out once and for all, and I was totally in agreement. But I asked if we could move the contest just around the corner into Dawlish Road where my mother couldn't see, because if she caught me actually fighting, she would give me one to be going on with. She was only five feet tall herself, but punched her weight. I was quick on my feet, but lacked her ring-craft.

Yorath cheered me up no end by saying that Bisto was a very good fighter, and would probably wallop me. I thanked him cordially for his confidence in me, but then I realised that I had never actually seen Bisto fight anybody. He was very good at threatening, and bullying, and sneaking upon you when you weren't looking; but I had never seen him put his fists up to anybody. They all took his bluster at face value, and believed that he really was a hard case. Suddenly I was utterly confident. I waded into Bisto, and gave him an awful pasting, and it was easy. His tough-guy image was sheer bravado, and when his nose began to bleed he backed off and hid behind a garden gate. So I gave Ginger Williams and one or two others a clout to keep their memories fresh, and put my jacket back on.

From that very moment I ceased to be a "Merrywood Sissy." I was now very definitely one of the boys, but I took great care not to crow too loudly. They were hard lads, in Lynton Road. Bisto said he would be only too delighted to have a return fight, only he had this mysterious ailment which made his nose bleed profusely if you so much as looked at it. But Yorath Davies had the last word. He said that my dad could probably knock out Tommy Farr as well, but not so quickly as his dad had done.

I rapidly settled down at school. Not only were Maurice Marks and some of the lads from Victoria Park there with me; notables like David "Henry" Herbert, Don Williams, David Gunning and "Jammer" James. There were good new friends like Bob Warren, John Young, and Michael Bush (another Country Bus boy, from Wrington).

And of course, there was Bob Flower. He was very bright, and was brave enough, in a city with two soccer teams of its own, to own up to being a fervent Arsenal supporter. When he played in first-year matches, he would wear white shorts right down to his kneecaps, and fatly padded socks, which overlapped the shorts. This, according to him, was what the well-dressed Arsenal player was wearing at the time. He took music lessons from Miss Chilcott in Hall Street. I joined him for a time, but I don't think there was any danger of either of us turning professional. I certainly didn't apply myself to school work as assiduously as I should have done, and it took me a year to resolve to stop enjoying school life for its own sake, and start the process of education in earnest. I was under-achieving, and didn't realise it until it was almost too late to catch up.

Bob and I used to go out for walks around Bedminster when he had finished his paper round. I envied him his wages, but there were no vacancies for paperboys in Lynton Road. Not only were there no newsagents close by, but not many people read newspapers; and if they did, the life expectancy of a paperboy in that area would be very short indeed. Usually we strolled as far as Bedminster Bridge, and studied the effluence flowing beneath with great interest. More than once, we promised each other that one day we would be back in Bedminster, and we would have enough money to buy all the property we took a fancy to. The bit in the middle, about how we were to obtain the money in the first place, was usually passed over without comment. Our young imaginations were being fired with ambition, but at present the flames were still flickering, and didn't seem to light the way to anywhere definite. But we were utterly certain that, as much as we respected our fathers, we certainly did not intend to sweep roads or drive a lorry for a living.

Christmas came and went, and as spring approached, the talk was all about how quickly the war would end. Allied bombers had destroyed whole German cities; the allies had crossed the Rhine, and the stories being told of the obscenities which had taken place in Nazi concentration camps, stories, which in spite of the hatred of the Germans which had been instilled in us for five years, were impossible to digest. There were rumours that Mussolini and Hitler were both dead, and that the war against Japan had turned in our favour. We knew that Mr. Churchill, Stalin and Roosevelt had met at somewhere called Yalta, to discuss how the dreadful, endless conflict should be wound up. The blackout was now at an end, and the bombing had ceased long ago. We used our Anderson shelter to store things in, and to grow marrows and rhubarb on; the beds inside had already been turned into sledges for when it snowed and we could use the Novers as a ski-slope.

On June 9th, the Allies landed in France on what they called "D-Day". We all knew it would happen soon. American troops were everywhere, and convoys of army lorries were regularly clogging the A38 out of Bristol. In October, British troops landed in Greece, and in November the Royal Air Force sank the mighty German battleship, the *Tirpitz*. Even now, some servicemen had been released early on compassionate grounds, and it was a fairly common sight to see a house decorated with the Union Jack, and bunting, and notices saying "Welcome Home, Jack!" or whoever.

But all these were just names and places to us; they meant very little to the younger lads at school, who had heard them repeated time after time so that they became part of our conversation without revealing the slightest clue as to their implications.

Lynton Road was now talking about how to celebrate the end of the war. Most people had come to live here from the old slums of Bristol, with narrow streets like Catherine Mead Street, where it was traditional to hang bunting and banners from one side to the other from opposite bedroom windows. They were used to erecting trestle tables on the cobbles, with chairs for the children, and doing so with no fear that passing traffic would be a problem, because there was no passing traffic. Lynton Road had no traffic to worry about, but the street was far too wide to allow a length of bunting to be stretched between houses. And the road was so long that, while you could be on the best of terms with neighbours up to a dozen houses away on each side, beyond that you scarcely knew people's names. In fact, there was none of the cosiness of the tiny, two up and two down houses which covered most of old Bedminster.

So the neighbours agreed to have a huge bonfire, on the allotments at the back of the houses and at the foot of the Novers. Everyone brought out anything they could spare and which was combustible. Long years of war meant that much of what could be burned had already gone up the chimney in the same way as coke, nutty slack, and logs dragged down from the Novers. Nevertheless, the pyre grew and grew, and somebody made an excellent effigy of Herr Hitler, put it in a wooden chair, and roped him to the top, black moustache and all. Amazingly, fireworks were becoming available, and the youths were already throwing bangers and

161

crackers at the girls in the street, while we youngsters looked on in astonishment at this phenomenon.

All we wanted now was a date, and at last it came.

On May 8th, 1945, the Allies accepted the unconditional surrender of all German forces, and the war in Europe was over.

29

I remember May 8th, 1945, very clearly indeed. I remember how people rejoiced all day, and how the church bells rang and the "All Clear" sirens sounded for the last time. I remember that the air seemed light, and folk walked around with a smile and a cheery word for anyone they passed. Visitors came and went in our house. Albert Mills from across the road came, straight from the Engineers' Arms, with the beer flopping about inside of him. He had been on leave when the war ended, and swore he wasn't going to bother to go back to his unit. He looked squiggle-eyed. He had a cigarette dangling from his lips, and sat at our old piano, and swayed as he vamped out all the wartime songs, tunes we had sung so many times in air raid shelters. There was no alcohol in our house, but it was readily available elsewhere; our callers made do with endless cups of my mother's tea. They talked and chattered excitedly as it grew darker, and the time for lighting the bonfire grew near. Mrs. Worgan, two doors away, had a son, Frank. He was a guardsman, and she was just bursting for him to come home after a tough time in Germany. She also had a son-in-law who was a sailor, and he, too had survived, and was in everybody's conversation. His war had included convoys to Russia through the frozen North Atlantic, and was too terrible to speak about. The lady over the road had a son in Burma, fighting the Japanese, and her delight at the end of the war in Europe was deadened by the knowledge that his war was far from finished.

We knew of one or two ladies in the street whose husbands had been away for years, and who had acquired other gentlemen friends in their absence. They had mixed feelings about peace descending upon the land. Some of them were confidently expecting to go to the United States with American boyfriends; but that night they mostly stayed at home. Others had young children who had never even seen their fathers, and these ladies were among the most excited of anybody.

We joined the growing crowd at the bonfire. My mother had Philip in her arms, and I kept an eye on David. George ran on

163

ahead and was full of information when we arrived. The fire would be lighted at any moment, and everybody would let fireworks off at the same time. This latter instruction had obviously been misunderstood by some of the wilder lads, because firecrackers and bangers were going off everywhere, and even the occasional rockets fizzed skywards. The fire gradually took hold, and orange flames licked up the timbers and turned yellow as they burst into the sky, sending sparks shooting still higher. Herr Hitler, on his wooden seat, lurched and fell backwards into the whirling flames, his coat blazing, and everyone roared in delight at this involuntary piece of symbolism. Rockets were screaming upwards every few seconds, guided out of the necks of milk bottles. Somebody had nailed some catherine wheels onto a plank, and they spun brightly to the delight of the youngest girls and boys. Someone began to sing, "There'll always be an England" and the crowd took it up with great fervour, and sang every patriotic song they could think of. When imaginations flagged, they turned to the National Anthem until fresh inspiration arrived and their combined repertoire was given full rein.

I was twelve years old now. I was fully aware of the excitement of the moment, and as thrilled as anybody by the blaze, the clamour, the singing, and the wild patriotism, enlivened by the horseplay led by Bisto Smith and his gang. But I was already lost in thought. I had retreated, as I often did, deep into my private inner self, and locked the world out. For the moment, I was unaware of all the euphoria. It was washing over me; I just wanted to think, as I gazed at the unfettered jubilation of those around me. I wandered up the Novers to the stone butt, and sat, and looked down on the tumultuous scene below, and pondered.

The flames were leaping, but during the bombing, I had seen leaping flames many times, and heard bangs, and shouts, and the frenzied singing of cowering people; except that now they were exultant. Then, they were terrified. Now, they were happy and triumphant.

I wondered how my father would be celebrating the end of the war. He certainly wouldn't be drinking; he never did. I was quite sure he would be thinking of us all, as we were of him. But I was doing my best to direct my mind to the future, and ignore the festivities around me. My mother had cared for us with fierce devotion and utter dedication for five years. We had never been hungry. We had certainly often been without many things we would have liked, but we never lacked anything we really needed. She had repaired our shoes on my father's three-legged cobbler's last. She had painted and decorated, kept the garden tidy, kept us clothed and made sure that we were well behaved. She had handled her small revenue brilliantly, had schemed, and innovated, had denied herself, taken in sewing, and had even worked as a charlady, to keep us comfortable. She had been a source of reassurance when we were distressed, and a fount of inspiration when we needed driving. She had been a mother and a father and a counsellor, and an example to us all; nobody could possibly have done more.

But, sooner or later, my father would be coming home, and would take over as the head of the family. Would he really want to, he whose life had been structured for him by King's Regulations for the last five years, so that he scarcely needed to make an independent decision? And would my mother be prepared to hand over the reins, after she had managed affairs so outstandingly on her own for such a long time?

My reveries were interrupted by a noise in the hedges, and the dreadful Alfie Brook dodged into view. He had a sickening, evil grin on his face, and he was pursued by an outraged Molly O'Grady. She screamed at him, something about money, and he distanced himself from her and was soon swallowed up in the crowd around the bonfire. She was carrying one shoe, and she perched on one leg as she tried to put it back on.

"That bastard!" she shrieked, "He owes I the money. If I catches up with'n, I'll scratch his bleedin' eyes out!" And she hobbled off as quickly as she could in the direction that Alfie had taken.

A young shape materialised, and perched itself beside me on the stone butt, his knees up to his chin and his arms gleefully clasping his legs; Bisto Smith.

"Good, innit?" he said.

"What is?" I asked.

"Well – thees know – all they fireworks, and the fire, and the singing and that. And Molly's out lookin' for Brooker because 'e 'ad 'er up the Novers again, an' never give 'er no money."

I could see what he meant, but I wished he would go away. I was still busy, trying to think my way through things, and to reach a

165

conclusion about what life might be like when all the jollities had been left behind, and everyone would need to plan a new style of living.

Suddenly there was a dreadful screech from the direction of the bonfire, followed by a roar of laughter from the crowd. Bisto was on his feet in an instant, and listening hard.

"Molly's caught Brooker! She'll kill'n! I ain't gonna miss this!" His disappeared abruptly, and I heard him crashing through the hedges, down towards the action, leaving me to make some sense of my half-formed philosophising.

There was one big problem which kept rising to the surface, and I found it very hard to frame in my mind. It was a matter of attitude, I supposed. Why was it that my family seemed to be reacting to the needs and requirements of other people all the time? Why was it expected that we would visit my Aunt's house every Boxing day for her party? Why was it that one of us had to struggle to British Road every time there was an air raid, to see if they were safe? Why did I perpetually resign myself to accepting the fact that if I wanted any equipment, I first had to ask myself if we could afford it? We usually couldn't, so I had to find the money somehow, and buy what I needed as cheaply as possible, and usually second-hand? Why did I have go to charity tea parties for kids whose fathers were away; or go on holiday in camps for the poor people; or receive other people's unwanted books and toys from organisations like the S.S.A.F.F.A.? And why did the difference between a very ordinary Christmas, and a Christmas with something a little extra, depend on the kindness of Mr. Payne and his annual ten-shilling note?

I knew it wasn't all a matter of being poor. And it certainly was not a symptom of helplessness, of being unable to live without handouts and support from other agencies. I gradually came to realise that it had a lot to do with my father's lifelong philosophy, that some were meant to command, but most of us were put on this earth to obey. "The rich man in his castle, The poor man at his gate." Everyone must know his place, my father had said many times. That was why he saw nothing unusual about winding up his war at exactly the same rank at which he began. He accepted that as the normal order of things, in his experience. Perhaps I would have thought so too, had I lived his life, in the terrible circumstances in which he was brought up. I looked down the hill towards the houses. The sky

166

above the roofs was flushed with scarlet from half a dozen fires like ours, all over Bedminster. People were still singing sporadically around our bonfire, fuelled regularly by late arrivals now returning from the Engineers' Arms. There were still explosions and intermittent bangs as people dug deep and found the last of their fireworks. There were even the odd stiff, white fingers of search-lights, criss-crossing the sky, as the military joined the civilians in their celebrations.

I was cold now. I had been sitting and thinking for so long that I was stiff, and my backside was numb from perching on the stone butt. I had solved nothing; but the realisation had dawned that the end of the war did not mark the beginning of paradise. There would be different problems to be faced, problems of a very complex nature. Somewhere, I had a place in their solution; but I couldn't yet work out where. I trotted down the muddy path and found my mother.